Teaching About The Constitution

Clair W. Keller
Denny L. Schillings
Editors

NATIONAL COUNCIL FOR THE SOCIAL STUDIES

Library of Congress Catalog Card Number 87-061298
ISBN 0-87986-055-3

3501 Newark Street, N.W., Washington, DC 20016

TABLE OF CONTENTS

CONTRIBUTORS

Herman Belz is Professor of History at the University of Maryland. He has written several books and articles that treat constitutional problems of the Civil War era and is co-author of *The American Constitution: Its Origins and Development* (Sixth Edition, 1983). He is currently engaged upon a study of recent civil rights policy, tentatively entitled, "Affirmative Action from Kennedy to Reagan: Redefining American Equality."

Bonny M. Cochran is a resource teacher and chairperson of the Social Studies Department at Bethesda-Chevy Chase High School in Bethesda, Maryland. She was a contributor to the *Social Studies Curriculum Materials Data Book* and the *Teacher's Guide for Teaching Ethnic Heritage Studies,* published by the Social Science Education Consortium, where she was a teacher associate from 1974–75.

Susan M. Darnley teaches social studies at South River High School in Edgewater, Maryland. She has co-authored a series of curriculum guides for Anne Arundel County Schools. She and colleague Rosemary V. Miller are co-authors of "Law-Related Education—Trends and Developments," and *Understanding Maryland Government.*

James A. Duea teaches high school social studies and is a K–12 social studies teacher specialist in the Ames Community Schools in Ames, Iowa. He has presented papers at state and regional social studies conferences.

Jill Louise Fernandez has recently completed her second year at the University of Washington Law School, where she is specializing in maritime law. She was formerly a research associate in the Boulder Valley Public Schools in Boulder, Colorado.

Clair W. Keller is Professor of History and Education at Iowa State University. The recipient of numerous academic honors, awards, and grants, he has published extensively on the teaching of United States history to high school students. His books include *Involving Students in the New Social Studies* and *Freedom's Trail,* an eighth-grade textbook co-authored with Richard Bartlett. He is a frequent presenter at annual meetings of the National Council for the Social Studies, the American Historical Association, and the Organization of American Historians. He served as president of the Iowa Council for the Social Studies from 1980–82 and was chairperson of SIGHT (Special Interest Group for History Teachers) from 1977–79.

Linda K. Kerber is May Brodbeck Professor in the Liberal Arts at the University of Iowa in Iowa City. She has written prolifically about the role of women in American history, particularly during the early federal period. This is the subject of one of her books, *Women of the Republic: Intellect and Ideology in Revolutionary America.* She is currently serving on the Executive Board of the Organization of American Historians and on the editorial boards of *Reviews in American History, Signs: A Journal of Women in Culture and Society,* and *Virginia Magazine of History and Biography.*

John W. Larner is serving as Editor for the Papers of Carlos Montezuma, the Papers of the Society of American Indians, and *The Osage Murders—A Documentary History.* He is Assistant Professor of History at the Pennsylvania State University at Altoona and has recently developed a packet of constitutional lessons for the Pennsylvania State Department of Education, *Pennsylvania and Constitutional Development, 1776-1794.*

Ronald Levitsky teaches seventh- and eighth-grade social studies at Sunset Ridge School in Northfield, Illinois. He has devised classroom simulations on the Supreme Court and the Civil War and has co-authored an article, "Supreme Court Simulation Game."

Donald S. Lutz is Professor of Political Science at the University of Houston. He is the author of six books and several dozen articles. His specialty is American political theory, especially the origin, operation, and theoretical content of American state and national constitutions. His primary commitment is to teaching, for which he has received a number of awards, and he currently serves as president of a local school board.

Fay Metcalf is Staff Director at the National Commission on the Social Studies in Washington, D.C. She previously served as Coordinator of the Center for Non-English Speaking Students in the Boulder Valley Schools, following 15 years as a classroom social studies teacher. She has published extensively on teaching about local history, minorities, and ethnicity in American society.

Howard N. Meyer is a former practicing labor attorney. He served as an aide to U.S. Attorneys General Francis Biddle and Tom Clark in the administrations of Franklin Roosevelt and Harry S Truman. He subsequently became a civil rights historian, concentrating on the relationship between black history and constitutional history. He has written books, essays, reviews, and a Pulitzer-nominated study that views American history in light of the rise, fall, and rebirth of the Fourteenth Amendment—*The Amendment That Refused to Die.*

Rosemary V. Miller teaches social studies at South River High School in Edgewater, Maryland. In addition to co-authoring a series of curriculum guides for Anne Arundel County Schools and a number of publications with colleague Susan M. Darnley, she has developed lessons on federalism and slavery, recently published by the Society for History Education.

Gordon Mixdorf teaches ninth-grade social studies and is co-chairperson of the Social Studies Department at West Senior High School in Iowa City, Iowa.

Under a grant from the Iowa Department of Public Instruction, he developed materials for students with learning disabilities or using English as a second language, and he has been a curriculum writer for the Iowa City School District since 1979.

Richard J. Morey teaches social studies and is chairperson of the Social Studies Department at Prairie School in Racine, Wisconsin. He served as a consultant to the National Street Law Institute in Washington, D.C., in the revision of the Lerner "Great Trials" series and co-authored an article, "Does the Constitution Protect the Despised?".

James J. Pyne teaches United States history at Homewood-Flossmoor High School in Flossmoor, Illinois, and is presently at work on a doctoral degree in American history at the University of Illinois-Chicago. He has co-authored "Activity and Study Skills," a booklet for use with *History of the United States* (Boorstin and Kelley).

Denny L. Schillings teaches social studies at Homewood-Flossmoor High School in Flossmoor, Illinois, and has co-authored a new high school textbook, *A World History.* He has developed a variety of curricular materials for teaching about the Constitution, has reviewed publications on Russia and the Soviet Union from the Russian Outreach Services of Harvard, Yale, and the University of Illinois, and has served as a contributor to or consultant for high school textbooks in economics, U.S. history, and European history. He currently serves on the NCSS Board of Directors, the Executive Board of the Illinois Council for the Social Studies, and the Board of Directors of the Illinois Association for the Advancement of History.

Michael Solliday is Associate Professor of Curriculum, Instruction and Media at Southern Illinois University at Carbondale and was formerly a classroom social studies teacher. He has served on the *Social Education* Editorial Board, in the NCSS House of Delegates, and as chairperson of the NCSS Teacher Education and Certification Committee. He was Executive Director of the Illinois Council for the Social Studies from 1978-86. His publications focus on the status of social studies education, and he has acted as a social studies consultant in many capacities.

Mary K. Bonsteel Tachau is Professor of History at the University of Kentucky. She was named one of the Outstanding Educators of America in 1972 and has received teaching and service awards, as well as numerous national research grants. Her book, *Federal Courts in the Early Republic: Kentucky 1789–1816,* won the Governor's Award of the Kentucky Historical Society in 1979. She has published extensively about early American history, Southern history, and Kentucky history.

Karen Tryda teaches seventh- and eighth-grade social studies at the Cleveland School of Science in Cleveland, Ohio. She has been active in developing social studies materials for use in the Cleveland Public Schools, including a curriculum guide for law-related education for grades 3–6.

Joseph L. White teaches social studies at Normal Community High School in Normal, Illinois, and is head of the Social Studies Department, McClean County Unit #5 (K–12 coordinator). He also teaches at Lincoln College in Lincoln, Illnois.

Stephanie Zaidman teaches courses in American history and the American legal system at Pilgrim High School in Warwick, Rhode Island. She has served as president of the Rhode Island Social Studies Association and has been a member of the NCSS Academic Freedom Committee since 1980.

INTRODUCTION

Clair W. Keller
and
Denny L. Schillings

In 1831, Alexis de Tocqueville observed that "scarcely any question arises in the United States which does not become, sooner or later, a subject of judicial debate. . . ." The United States Constitution and the interpretations of it by the Supreme Court often lie at the center of that judicial debate. It is a tribute to the flexibility of the Constitution that it has survived, and in 1987, its 200th anniversary is occasion for great national celebration.

When we proposed this Bulletin to NCSS, we wanted to accomplish several things. First of all, we intended to provide scholarly historical perspectives on the changing nature of the Constitution and the society in which it has prevailed. For ease of organization and usability, we decided upon a chronological format. The book opens with a discussion of constitutionalism in the abstract and progresses through the eighteenth, nineteenth, and twentieth centuries, presenting a general overview of significant concepts or interpretations for each period. The essays are not meant to be definitive, but rather are intended to provide a focus and a point of departure for further study.

Secondly, we wanted to equip teachers with material about the Constitution that could be of immediate use in the classroom. The teaching activities that accompany the historical overviews provide a variety of approaches to classroom instruction. They suggest a wide range of classroom options, from role-playing, to script-reading, to case study. The lack of a common structure was intended to allow individual authors to determine the form, content, and use of the activities.

It was our hope to avoid repeating material that would be available in numerous other sources; thus, we have included no specific activity on the Bill of Rights. On the other hand, we wanted to provide activities that would help teachers to bring into focus the contributions and exasperations of blacks, women, and others whom the framers ignored. The Constitution, like all human endeavors, is and was, as George Washington wrote, ". . . not free from imperfections. . . ." Questions of slavery and suffrage, for example, were left to future generations.

Finally, we wanted to include a bibliography that would make a conscious and consistent effort to focus on the classroom teacher and student. There are several lengthy and excellent bibliographies devoted to the Constitution. The annotated bibliography developed for this book is of moderate length. Its special contribution is that it not only summarizes content, but also discusses possible uses of the materials as primary and supplementary classroom reading. We hope that this feature will make it particularly valuable to social studies teachers and students alike.

We believe that there is a great deal of good material in these pages, at the same time that we recognize that there are many aspects and issues that we have not explored. If social studies educators find something of value and usefulness here, we will be amply rewarded for our efforts.

Earlier versions of Chapter 2, "Writing and Ratifying the Constitution," by Linda K. Kerber, and three of the teaching activities that follow it were developed with the assistance of the Rockefeller Foundation and the Johnson Foundation, for an American Historical Association conference series funded by the National Endowment for the Humanities. These three activities are: "A Do-It-Yourself Constitution," by Denny L. Schillings; "Black People and the Constitution," by Bonny M. Cochran and Linda K. Kerber; and "The Path to Political Power for Women," by Bonny M. Cochran. We are grateful to the organizations whose sponsorship and support helped to produce this work.

Last of all, we want to extend a special thanks to the National Council for the Social Studies for recognizing the need for this book and providing a means for it to reach the classroom.

Part I

The Eighteenth Century

CHAPTER I

THE ORIGINS OF AMERICAN CONSTITUTIONALISM

Donald S. Lutz

The bicentennial of the American founding era has given rise to renewed interest in the origins and fundamental commitments of American constitutional thought. One aspect of this has been heightened attention to a difficult matter that has engrossed historians and political scientists for a good number of years—the identification of the various intellectual traditions upon which American constitutionalism draws, and the influence of these various traditions on the United States Constitution.

The arguments advanced by the framers and justifiers of the Constitution were derived in part from the historical experience of the colonies and the concrete facts of their political situation as a new nation. In part, they resulted from deep reflection on the ends of republican government. The latter enterprise has been known since its origin in classical Greece as political philosophy. The Constitution thus resulted from a prolonged, manifold discussion which both reflected and advanced a 2,000-year-old conversation on the nature of good government.

Even well-prepared students in introductory-level college American government and American history courses sometimes display a profound ignorance not only of the principles and workings of the Constitution, but also of the connection of the Constitution to a "way of life" chosen by serious men after long deliberation. In part, this reflects the fact that in recent decades political scientists have largely ignored the philosophical background—instead, for example, undertaking a more narrow and technical consideration of the design and operation of congress or the presidency. In addition, many historians have been inclined to view constitutional design as simply the result of competing ideologies, and thus of competing interests, rather than as an expression of careful theoretical thinking. High school teachers who have taken the trouble to acquaint themselves with academic writing on the subject have found, until recently, little to help them in understanding the intellectual foundations of the Constitution.

A quarter of a century ago consideration of the origins of the Constitution was dominated by three competing positions. The first, exemplified by the writing of Charles Beard, argued that the Constitution resulted from and reflected the economic interests of a particular class among the several classes competing for political power in late eighteenth-century America. Already partially discredited by the 1950s and severely restricted thereafter, Charles Beard's position is still prominently displayed in most major high school textbooks—a testament to the dominance of this position in the recent past.

A second position, exemplified by the work of Louis Hartz, held that American political thought, and thereby the United States Constitution, was thoroughly dominated by the work of John Locke. High school textbooks still emphasize Locke's influence, often by lining up quotes from Locke side by side with passages from American founding documents.

The third position, exemplified by the work of Daniel Boorstin, held that no coherent theory had been successfully transplanted from Europe to America. Boorstin argued that Americans were a pragmatic people shaped by the necessities and opportunities of their environment. Boorstin's own textbook is currently one of the most widely used at the high school level, attesting to the continuing influence of his position.

Recent research has reaffirmed the importance of John Locke, just as it has shown the importance of economic conditions and political events in America to the design of the Constitution. At the same time, the influences upon the American constitutional tradition are far more diverse and complex than the dominant positions of the 1950s imply. An emerging consensus among academicians studying the American founding does not so much reject these three positions as place them in a broader context, thus diminishing the relative importance of each. At the same time, research over the past quarter of a century indicates the need for much closer attention to the philosophical underpinnings of the Constitution.

The consensus emerging from recent work can be summarized in the following manner:

1. Of all political phenomena that can be studied, constitutions are the most likely to be ones where ideas and theories make a difference. Both the nature of the enterprise of constitutional design, and the characteristics of those doing the designing, ensure that philosophical considerations will be prominent.
2. Circumstances surrounding its writing, and the quality of its framers, ensured that the United States Constitution would be especially theoretical in its origin and content.
3. Although certain important aspects of the Constitution, such as the three-fifths compromise, can be explained by reference to social and political circumstances, the architectonic design of the document, as well as its fundamental commitments, can be explained to a large extent only by reference to theoretical and philosophical principles.
4. The Constitution in its various provisions reflects the influence of the biblical covenant tradition, colonial political experience, English Whig political theory, the English common law tradition, and a host of writers associated with the Scottish Enlightenment and various phases of the Enlightenment on the European continent.
5. The United States Constitution draws upon a variety of theoretical sources, but it is not merely derivative. Rather, it is a historically important synthesis

that produced a highly principled, coherent political philosophy that is distinctively American.

Heated debate is currently being waged over how to describe or categorize the various strands of influence, their relative influence, what specifically was borrowed or derived from each, the precise nature of the resulting synthesis, and the terms of its commitments. The outpouring of books and articles has been so overwhelming in recent years, the number of possible influences are so many, and the tendency for authors to consider only a small part of the picture has been so pronounced, that at first the subject looks like a classic case of academic anarchy. The situation is not as desperate as it seems, however, and order can be brought to the literature by recognizing a few simple facts.

The first fact is that the United States Constitution did not suddenly spring from the heads of fifty-five men in Philadelphia, in a historical vacuum. The Constitution was written to overcome the inadequacies of an earlier national constitution—the Articles of Confederation. It was also written to modify the effects of state constitutions that had already been in effect for several years. Put another way, the United States Constitution was at least the eighteenth constitution written and adopted by Americans since the onset of the Revolution. It both borrowed from and reacted to the earlier documents.

These earlier constitutions themselves made reference to documents of political foundation written by the colonists. Indeed, Massachusetts, Connecticut, and Rhode Island continued living under colonial documents after 1776 as if they were constitutions. We can trace constitutional development back a hundred and fifty years in America before the Philadelphia convention.

The straightforward linkage between the United States Constitution and colonial documents of foundation means that our constitutional tradition was an extension of European political thought, as well as of experience upon our own shores. Americans were part of the British constitutional system before the war for independence. As a consequence, the debate between England and America during 1762–1776 often took the form of argument over constitutional interpretation, rather than of disputation between opposing political theories.

We can look upon American constitutionalism as proceeding through a series of historical "frames," with each frame representing a successive stage of development. The earlier frames condition the latter ones in the sense of delimiting, but not determining, the influences on evolving American constitutional theory. This idea will be clarified in subsequent discussion. For now, recognizing that American constitutionalism had a long history that passed through several stages before 1787 will allow us to appreciate the possibility that the various influences upon American constitutionalism were not all *prominent* in 1787, but had been introduced at various times over a long development. Among other things, we need to distinguish constitutional theory during the middle 1770s from that during the late 1780s. The Declaration of Independence is part of the general development, but the influences prominent in 1776 were not the same as those prominent during 1787.

We can identify five frames of influence within which we can place all the various writers and intellectual traditions that have been identified by historians and political scientists as relevant to the American Constitution:

1. The colonial charters
2. The English common law
3. The foundation documents written by the colonists, including the Declaration of Independence
4. The early state constitutions and the debates surrounding their writing
5. The debates leading up to and surrounding the U.S. Constitution

Between 1578 and 1732 dozens of charters were written granting or regranting land in America to English settlers. These charters varied considerably in purpose, content, and form, but most of them shared two historically important features. First of all, they provided for local self-government as long as the laws passed were not contrary to the laws of England. Second, they declared that the settlers in America would have the same "Liberties, Franchises, and Immunities" as those still residing in England. The first provision allowed the colonists to develop a rich experience in designing their own political institutions, writing their own laws, and running their own political systems. It is difficult to imagine Americans writing successful constitutions in the 1770s and 1780s without the previous century and a half of experience in institutional design. They would not have had this experience without the standard provision in the charters for local self-government.

The provision granting full English citizenship to the colonists and their descendents had the effect of transmitting to American shores all of the English common law, including the centerpiece of this tradition—the Magna Carta. Unlike the Spanish and French colonists, the English colonists were full participants in the constitutional system of the mother country. Throughout the colonial era, the colonists in America used their common law rights to protect their interests. The provisions of the Magna Carta shaped their legal arguments vis-á-vis the mother country during debates over charter revision, during the constant struggles between crown-appointed governors and colonial-elected legislatures, during the Stamp Act crisis, and finally during the crisis that led to independence. Together with the political theory developed during their colonial experience of self-rule, the Americans relied upon English common law to structure their position justifying independence and to justify the form taken by the constitutions they wrote when newly independent. The charters were the first frame of influence. Without them and the specific form they took, American constitutionalism would not be what it is today—if indeed we could have had an independent constitutional tradition.

Since all English colonists operated under one charter or another, they became accustomed to having a single piece of paper serve as their founding document. These charters were from time to time revised or replaced. In the 1770s and 1780s Americans would invent the modern constitution. It would be contained in a single written document and be amendable or replaceable through a process specified in the document. It is difficult not to see the form of American constitutions as indebted in at least this respect to the colonial charters.

However, throughout the colonial era, Americans were subject to two sets of documents. The first set was comprised of those documents, such as the charters, written in England. The second set was comprised of those written by themselves under the charter provision for local self-government. The

Mayflower Compact, the Pilgrim Code of Law, the Fundamental Orders of Connecticut, and the Massachusetts Body of Liberties are only the best known of several hundred such documents of foundation written in America. Although not always honored in practice, these documents developed and enshrined the ideas of popular sovereignty, political equality, majority rule, representation, and several other principles which are central to our constitutional tradition.

These documents in turn derived to a significant degree from the form and content of religious covenants. For example, the Mayflower Compact is a church covenant in which a civil body politic is created instead of a church. Church covenants became civil covenants, which evolved into compacts, which in turn evolved into constitutions. Many of the early state constitutions written between 1776 and 1787 were compacts, now called constitutions, which could be traced back through the documentary history of their respective colonies to religious covenants.

The use of covenants to establish political systems in turn derived from the Protestant appropriation of the Jewish concept as found in the Bible. Calvinist theology stressed the centrality of the Bible, and the Protestants settling North American shores were overwhelmingly from such Calvinist denominations. Their religion led them not only to adopt and adapt the biblical convenant idea to political ends, but also to adopt certain political principles, such as political equality. Accepting the notions that all individuals are made in the image and likeness of God and that all individuals are equally capable of and responsible for their own actions, it was but a small step to viewing all individuals as having a rough political equality and regarding the consent of each as having equal status. It is difficult to underestimate the influence of the biblically derived foundation documents written by colonial Americans upon the development of American constitutionalism. Religion would continue to inform American political action during the revolutionary era, both in justifying the grounds for the break with England, and in suggesting principles of institutional design for the state constitutions. The Bible, Calvin, and colonial documents would also structure the manner in which English common law was appropriated.

The English common law transmitted to the colonists by the charters was an amorphous mass of legal cases stretching back for centuries. However, even as the colonies were being founded, Sir Edward Coke was publishing his *Institutes,* which codified the common law. Moreover, his codification argued the case for the monarch being limited in power by the common law, especially by the Magna Carta. Coke was widely read in America for well over a century, until 1772, when Blackstone's *Commentaries* were published in the colonies and became the primary link with the common law. Under Coke's tutelage, the Americans added to their constitutional tradition the notion of government being limited by law. They also learned from Coke how to use bills of rights to codify these limits. The Americans, however, were highly selective in what they appropriated from the Magna Carta and the common law. Most of it had to do with feudal relationships and the rights of the aristocracy relative to the king. These parts the colonists pointedly ignored.

The right of trial by a jury of one's peers; the right to a speedy trial; prohibitions on bills of attainder, ex post facto laws, and cruel and unusual punishment; the guarantee of habeas corpus; and the notion of equal protection under the laws—these were retained from the common law. Most importantly, the colonists drew from the Magna Carta the fundamental principle of no taxation without the consent of those being taxed. This common law principle was generalized in America to the principle that all government should be based upon consent. The colonists adopted the portion of English common law that was congruent with the principles and practices derived from their religious commitments and their colonial institutional development. They excluded anything else. In this fashion, the early "frames of influence" structured those that followed and continued to influence the development of American constitutionalism.

Colonial politics, as one might expect, revolved around the relationship of the colonists to Britain. Sometimes political issues concerned this relationship directly. For example, several times England tried to bring the colonies under more direct control by making them all royal colonies or by finding new ways to tax them. However, more often than not, this relationship was addressed indirectly by focusing upon the power struggle between the legislatures, which were elected by the colonists, and the governors, who in all but a few cases were appointed by the crown. This struggle during the first half of the eighteenth century led eventually to the legislatures' gaining the upper hand, and had much to do with American preference for legislative supremacy in their early state constitutions.

Along the way, several other institutions characteristic of American constitutional design were developed. Most prominent among these was the notion of separation of powers. The crown-appointed governors had used every means at their disposal to gain the upper hand in the struggle with their respective colonial legislatures. One widely used tactic was to appoint members of the legislature to offices which paid a stipend. With enough members of the legislature being at least in part financially dependent upon the governor, the governor could then expect a more docile legislature. The colonists responded by prohibiting multiple office-holding. They called this "separation of powers," and it meant simply that when someone was elected to the legislature, he had to resign any positions under the executive, or having once accepted such a paying position, he had to resign from the legislature. From such modest political beginnings did Americans evolve the great architectonic device of separation of powers for their constitutions.

In their struggles with the British government, the Americans were aided by the ideas of the English Whigs. Emerging in the turmoil of the Commonwealth period in England, the Whigs were the loyal opposition during the early part of the eighteenth century in England. They were concerned with increasing the strength of Parliament vis-á-vis the monarch, enhancing representation, especially through the elimination of rotten burroughs, and extending the rights of social classes other than the aristocracy. John Locke was perceived by the colonists as a member of this group. Locke, Algernon Sidney, and Cato (Trenchard and Gordon) were widely read and cited from 1760 onward. Other

English Whig writers included Bishop Hoadley, Bolingbroke, Price, Burgh, Milton, Rollin, Molesworth, Priestly, Macauley, Somers, Harrington, and Rapin.

Aside from Locke and Harrington, these names would be recognizable to few today, although some would correctly suspect that this was the Milton who wrote *Paradise Lost.* As a group, these English Whigs had much to say that was congruent with what Americans were already doing or wanted to do. They provided a sound justification and deep theoretical reasoning for American institutions already in existence. The debates surrounding the writing of the state constitutions between 1776 and 1787 were considerably enriched and advanced by reference to the English Whigs. Their influence was so marked during this period of American constitutionalism that many Americans working and writing in support of republican institutions called themselves Whigs to signify their attachments and intellectual debts.

In addition, the ideas of Locke and Sidney figured prominently in the literature justifying the break with England. Locke's work gives profound consideration to the bases for establishing a government and for opposing tyranny, but has little to say about designing institutions. Therefore, his contributions to American political thought were in justifying the Revolution and the right of Americans to write their own constitutions, rather than in the design of any state or national constitutions. The Declaration of Independence sounds derivative from Locke, but in fact reads much like any number of colonial documents written just before or after Locke was born. An examination of the Pilgrim Code of Law (1636) is instructive in this regard. Locke and the other English Whigs had their greatest influence on American constitutionalism between 1765 and 1780, when they were fitted into the earlier frames of influence. Put another way, the reason that Locke was so widely quoted at the time had more to do with his providing a justification for American theory and institutions already in place, than with the sheer power or novelty of his ideas. He and the English Whigs helped to develop and deepen American constitutionalism, but in directions already set by the earlier frames of influence.

Another group of writers became prominent during the debates surrounding the writing of the state constitutions, and they would be central to the debate surrounding the writing and adoption of the United States Constitution. We speak of them today as members of the European Enlightenment, as if they comprised a single, coherent group. While a commitment to rational analysis characterized this group as a whole, it was nonetheless composed of a very diverse set of thinkers, and there are recognizable sub-groupings which fit into American political thought in different ways.

The ideas of the so-called Scottish Enlightenment came early to America in the writings of Francis Hutcheson and stayed late in the writings of David Hume. Francis Hutcheson was prominent in the college readings of many who would help write the national Constitution. His major work appeared in 1725, and by the time he was read by people like Jefferson and Madison, Hutcheson's ideas were commonplace in English and American thinking. His influence tended to reinforce what Americans were already thinking about constitutional design. On the other hand, David Hume's work began to be cited prominently around 1780, and his influence moved thinking on constitutional design to a new level and helped introduce significant innovation.

Enlightenment writers of other stripes tended to fall into these same two categories—those who largely reinforced ideas and institutions already accepted in America, and those who helped to introduce innovation into the ongoing development of American constitutionalism. The most widely cited European thinker during the entire founding era was Montesquieu, whose ideas primarily supported well-understood positions. The same was true for Pufendorf, Grotius, Rousseau, Raynal, Mably, Burlamaqui, and Vattel. This is not to say that these men lacked original ideas, or had nothing of value to add, but that they were appropriated selectively by American thinkers to support their positions about American constitutional design. The Americans borrowed from these Enlightenment thinkers to deepen the theoretical synthesis already in progress. That both Federalists and Anti-federalists drew about evenly from these men indicates how they were used. The view that the Federalists used Enlightenment thinkers to advance beyond the more traditional view held by the Anti-federalists contains a grain of truth that is confused by a misnomer.

The misnomer results from a practice of identifying many writers with the Enlightenment who belong properly to another category. It is also useful to note that the recent practice of placing European thinkers into one of several broad categories is itself not always helpful. Rather than assigning to categories the men whose ideas fostered innovation in late eighteenth-century American constitutional design, it is more useful simply to note that they all shared a desire to develop a science of human and political behavior. Isaac Newton and Francis Bacon were foremost in this group, Condorcet was the most avid practitioner, and Hume was the most successful conduit to America. The names are too numerous to mention them all, but men like Hutcheson, Adam Smith, Hobbes, Locke, Montesquieu, Burlamaqui, Adam Ferguson, and Beccaria all contributed to the notion that politics could be reduced to a science. Aside from Hume, whose influence on the minds of men like Madison may have been decisive, there are no specific names to which we can point. Still, the notion of viewing politics as following laws much the way nature follows the laws of Newtonian mechanics was more influential in the evolution of American constitutionalism than has usually been credited by historians and political scientists.

Thomas Jefferson was one of the first to adopt this stance. The contents of the Declaration of Independence were not new or startling for the time, but the language used by Jefferson reflected something other than Whig political thought. The opening sentence reads in part, "When in the course of human events it becomes necessary. . . ." In his *Principia,* Newton discerned necessity at work in seemingly random events. There were patterns that were invariable and predictable. A relatively few principles could be used to derive, in proper combination according to the circumstances, virtually all movements in the heavens. Things took their "course," to reach predictable outcomes or "events."

Hobbes had begun his *Leviathan* with a conception of human nature predicated upon a few principles of motivation which serve as "levers and wheels" to explain human action. The notion of "passions" or "interests" came to represent the core of a human nature whose actions were predictable under certain circumstances. The *Federalist Papers* by Hamilton, Madison, and Jay are full of scientific terms such as "tendency," "experiment," and even "political science." The term "revolution" did not have the meaning we attach to it today, but instead derived from the notion of the earth revolving upon its axis or making a revolution around the sun, thus implying gradual but inevitable change. A careful reading of the Federalists shows them tending to view constitutional design as a matter of responding to political, economic, and social circumstances as conditions for determining which principles of scientific design to use to direct human behavior to a desired goal.

The ideas about an extended republic, the size of the legislature, and the division of governmental powers to set "ambition against ambition"—the concept of checks and balances—all reflect the influence of Hume or the scientific perspective. Although the Federalists were quite innovative, they could not begin anew, but had to find a way to insert their principles of design into the context established by earlier frames of influence. As a result, there is surprising continuity between the United States Constitution and the institutions and practices developed in the early state constitutions and during the colonial period.

There has been no shortage of writing about the United States Constitution over the past two hundred years. It is surprising, therefore, that only recently have scholars undertaken the task of systematically unraveling the origins of the document. That process involves more than simply examining the document itself, since it is only part of a constitutional tradition that begins well before 1787. The overview here not only simplifies the problem, because of limited space, but also implies that we are more certain about origins than is the case. A revolution is going on in our view of the Constitution—a revolution that has been under way for at least two decades. There is a need to introduce our students to the richness and diversity that characterizes the ongoing search for an understanding of American constitutionalism in which we can have full confidence. It is unlikely that we will achieve such confidence until the present generation of high school students has had a chance to contribute to the effort.

CHAPTER 2

WRITING AND RATIFYING THE CONSTITUTION

Linda K. Kerber

The Constitutional Convention is one of the great "set-pieces" of the standard American history textbook. Virtually every text currently in use can be relied upon to offer the basic information: the dates of the Philadelphia meeting (May 25–September 17, 1787), the major patterns of debate (the Virginia Plan, the New Jersey Plan, the conflicting interests of small and large states, slave and free states, North and South), and the major patterns of compromise (on representation, the slave trade, the presidency). Because we know how effectively the Constitution has worked—with of course, the major exception of the Civil War—it is sometimes hard to avoid teaching it as a set of rules and regulations, rather than as one set of options chosen over other alternatives. Moreover, it is tempting to give most of our attention to the Federalists, the people who prevailed.

It requires a major effort of historical imagination to think of the political struggle as one which did not have to turn out the way it did. If we are to avoid portraying the founders as gods, we need to show students that reasonable people could disagree about the strengths and weaknesses of the constitutional compromises. We hope that students will emerge with the understanding that Anti-federalists as well as Federalists were reasonable, making choices that were justifiable under the circumstances in which they perceived themselves to be.

FEDERALISTS AND ANTI-FEDERALISTS

Federalists and Anti-federalists had much in common. Both had cast their lot with the republic rather than the British empire; both were patriots rather than Tories. They had lived under the government of the Articles of Confederation, which, whatever its defects, had sustained the republic through a successful revolution. In the 1780s, however, Federalists and Anti-federalists differed on the matter of how much energy and power invested in the central government would be compatible with the continued vitality of state and local government and with individual liberties.

Federalists and Anti-federalists made their decisions on the Constitution on the basis of abstract principles and personal experience. As Madison said in *Federalist* #10, "As long as the reason of man continues fallible, and he is at liberty to exercise it, different options will be formed. As long as the connection subsists between his reason and his self-love, his opinions and his passions will have a reciprocal influence on each other. . . ."

Recent scholarship has stressed at least three major themes in analyzing the intentions of Federalists and Anti-federalists.

First, Federalists and Anti-federalists often differed in the nature of their political experience. Some twenty-five years ago, in an essay called "The Founding Fathers: Young Men of the Revolution," Stanley Elkins and Eric McKitrick suggested that many leading Federalists had served in the Continental Army or the Continental Congress during the war years. In either capacity, they would have felt great frustration when states failed to meet their allocations of soldiers or of funds. Many of these men emerged from the war predisposed to believe that major revisions should be made in the Articles of Confederation. They concluded that a more "energetic" national government was needed, with more power over the states. They felt vindicated when Shays' Rebellion erupted in western Massachusetts and the Confederation seemed helpless to contain it. A people who had successfully staged one revolution against Britain could well be expected to mount other rebellions against their own government when displeased. What would halt an endless cycle of rebellions, if there were not a powerful national government? "One revolution," observed a Massachusetts Federalist wearily, "is enough for any man." In what was a successful public relations ploy, nationalists seized the label of Federalists, which in its strict definition would have better suited their opponents, and made it work for themselves.

Anti-federalists were likely to be men such as Patrick Henry, who had made their political careers in their own states—as members of state militias or in state or county politics. They were likely to be proud of their local governments, which had, after all, maintained order through the bitter years of war. They were likely to harbor some resentment against men in the Continental Congress or Army who had made demands on the states for soldiers, material, and money without much regard for the stress that these demands caused.

Secondly, Federalists and Anti-federalists often differed as to where they lived and how they made their livelihood. The differences were *not* simple ones between rich and poor, nor were they, as Charles Beard once argued, between those who held land and those who speculated in bonds. Support for Federalism seems to have been strongest in cities and the nearby countrysides which depended on the cities' commercial connections. Merchants and artisans—wealthy or struggling—could perceive that their economic self-interest lay with the development of a vigorous trade and a strong national government which could negotiate favorable commercial treaties. Anti-federalism seems to have been strong in the interior, where the demands of a coastal metropolis, like Boston, New York, or Philadelphia, seemed intrusive and irrelevant. It is important to note, however, that even this generalization breaks down in frontier areas like back-country Georgia, where settlers hoped for greater support in their fight against Indians. There was strong support for the Constitution here.

Political alignments were often shaped by personal experience. Patrick Henry, as an aggressive planter making his fortune, often found himself opposed—before and throughout the war—to men of old wealth and elite status—James Madison and Thomas Jefferson among them. He may well have been predisposed to oppose the Constitution because men he had long distrusted were supporting it. A similar pattern can be found in New York, where George Clinton and Abraham Yates had worked with members of the patriot elite, like Robert R. Livingston and Alexander Hamilton, and could clearly perceive the distrust that Livingston and Hamilton had for common people. Clinton was likely, for good reason, to be skeptical of whatever Livingston supported. The traditional principle, "The enemy of my enemy is my friend," explains a great many of the political alignments of 1788.

Finally, Federalists and Anti-federalists differed in their estimation of the risk associated with the proposed changes. It is important that students understand that most Anti-federalists were *not* absolutely opposed to the Constitution; indeed, many Anti-federalists were prepared to agree that major changes in the Articles of Confederation were in order. Yet, they deeply distrusted some aspects of the document they were asked to approve. They identified some issues which are serious concerns and with which we still wrestle today. Among their criticisms were at least three which are worth calling to students' attention.

1. Anti-federalists expressed distrust of the three-fifths compromise.
2. Anti-federalists were likely to think that the powers given to the President were excessive.
3. Finally, and most significantly, Anti-federalists were dismayed at the absence of a Bill of Rights.

It has been no small matter for the future development of the United States that Anti-federalists were successful in bargaining for the addition of the first ten amendments.

BLACK PEOPLE AND THE CONSTITUTION

The framers were self-conscious about slavery; the word was not used in the Constitution. But the issue entered emphatically into debates on representation, taxation, commercial regulation, domestic tranquility, state sovereignty, and interstate relations. The Constitution forbade states from passing laws which would free fugitives "held to service or labor" in another state. Representatives in Congress were to be allocated and direct taxes assessed on the basis of the population of all whites and three-fifths of persons "other than free." The international slave trade was to be permitted to continue for another 20 years, and was placed explicitly under Congressional jurisdiction. In these ways, the language of the Constitution recognizes that it was drafted for a society which included slaves and expected slavery to continue. When, a half-century later, William Lloyd Garrison would cry that the Constitution was a covenant with the Devil, it was this recognition that he had in mind.

The treatment of slavery in the Constitution reveals ambivalence in the attitudes of the framers toward slavery—an ambivalence shared by the Continental Congress. While the framers were debating in Philadelphia, the Continental Congress passed the Northwest Ordinance, excluding slavery from the territory north of the Ohio, but also including a fugitive slave clause.

Had the three-fifths ratio devised by framers of the Constitution ever been implemented in figuring direct taxes, it would have worked to the disadvantage of the slave states. However, taxes were never levied on the basis of the three-fifths clause; thus, slaveholders benefitted from the clause in increased representation, without having to pay any price.

Other clauses were ambiguous as well. Article IV, for example, requires that "Full Faith and Credit shall be given in each State to the public Acts, Records, & judicial Proceedings of every other State." Was this intended to mean that free states had to recognize the slave status of servants traveling with their masters? Some years later, when a former Mississippi slave living in Ohio was bequeathed substantial property by her white father, the executor of the Mississippi will refused to transmit the legacy, claiming that according to Mississippi law she was still a slave. In such a situation, which state was bound to give "full faith and credit" to the acts of the other?

Because most regulations about slavery were left to the states, the states were free to alter or abolish slavery. Many northern states had in fact already done so. The Constitution of Vermont had abolished slavery in 1777. In Massachusetts, the courts interpreted the state constitution as prohibiting slavery, and as early as 1790 there were no slaves to be counted in the census. Gradual manumission laws were passed in Pennsylvania in 1780, and in Rhode Island and Connecticut in 1784. The trend continued after the inauguration of the federal government. Slavery was abolished by the Constitution of Ohio in 1802; by gradual manumission laws in New York in 1799 (and in 1817) and in New Jersey in 1804.

But each gradual manumission law had its own complexities, and all left many older blacks enslaved for the rest of their lives. Masters could evade the requirement that youthful slaves be freed at a certain age by selling these slaves *before* they reached that age. The fugitive slave clause of the Constitution implied, and the Fugitive Slave Law of 1793 provided, that masters could pursue runaways and demand state help in recapturing them. Other slaves who entered free territory were not fugitives. They were brought there by masters who were traveling. A master could surely take a slave *into* a free state, but did it necessarily follow that the master could take the slave *out?* The answer to this question varied. In Connecticut, state law explicitly permitted out-of-state visitors to take slaves in and out of the state until the 1830s, but Pennsylvania law permitted sojourners to keep slaves only for six months, after which they were freed. Some northern states passed their own statutes which made it difficult to recapture a fugitive, but were in turn outwitted by the federal Fugitive Slave Act of 1850.

Most slaves were prohibited from learning about the Constitution. But by its implicit and explicit recognition of slavery, and by the ways in which the courts interpreted provisions like the fugitive slave clause and the "full faith and credit clause," the Constitution did a great deal to define the social and political matrix in which the slave system flourished.

Free black people, even though not enslaved themselves, lived in a social environment in which slavery lurked, coloring their relations with whites, limiting their options, and affecting their future. New York City, for example, where slavery persisted into the early nineteenth century, was far less hospitable to free blacks than Philadelphia, where slavery was eliminated in 1780.

Free black people lived in a world segregated by custom as well as law. Only white men could enlist in the militia; only white men could deliver mail. Free blacks could not vote in many free states; until 1849, black people—slave or free—could not testify against whites in Ohio courts. Blacks were unwelcome in public schools, in the seats of public omnibuses (they might, however, stand) and in the cabins of steamboats (they might stand on the exposed deck). One French traveller observed in the 1830s that evidence of the American belief that "God himself separated the white from the black" was to be found everywhere—"in the hospitals where humans suffer, in the churches where they pray, in the prisons where they repent, in the cemeteries where they sleep the eternal sleep." (Gustave de Beaumont, *Marie, or Slavery in the United States* Stanford, 1958, p. 66).

THE POLITICAL LOYALTIES OF WOMEN

The Constitution is expressed in the name of the people. It is the "people" of the United States who are said to "ordain and establish." Clearly, the framers exercised a certain amount of poetic license: All of the individuals alive in the new republic in 1787 did not gather to commission and approve the document. Who, precisely, were the historical actors who did the ordaining?

We can identify three groups of people. There were the men who met at Philadelphia. They were chosen by their state legislatures. There were the men who met in state ratification conventions, to vote for or against the Constitution. And, finally, there were the men who *voted* for delegates to the state ratification conventions. Federalists had insisted on bypassing the state legislatures and holding special conventions which could have only the Constitution on the agenda. They had wanted this in part because they feared that the vested interests of state legislators would incline them against the Constitution. Federalists also wished to establish the fitness of approving fundamental federal law in a more dedicated and thoroughgoing manner than ordinary legislation; there was to be a difference between statutes and constitutions. The people were the "constituent power"; in some sense, the Constitution had to be submitted to them.

The members of the ratification conventions were chosen by what was probably the largest electorate in the early republic. In New York at this time, for example, property qualifications usually limited those eligible to vote for the assembly to 58 percent of adult white males. Ordinarily, only 29 percent of adult white males were eligible to vote for senators and governor. In 1788, however, New York permitted universal male suffrage for the ratification convention. Not all men took advantage of their voting privilege, but the electorate seems to have been markedly larger, ranging from 5 percent to 30 percent in different counties. It is important to note that New York was exceptional; many other states simply allowed those normally eligible to vote to participate in elections for delegates to the ratification conventions. In those states, property requirements remained in effect, excluding a substantial proportion of adult men.

But even with universal suffrage, many adults remained excluded from the political community. Non-citizens—slaves and Native Americans—were excluded. Some citizens were also excluded—children, idiots, the insane, those in prison, and all women. We still find it sensible to exclude children, the insane, and the imprisoned from the electorate. Why did the founders think it was common sense to exclude women?

The exclusion of married women from the vote was based on the same principle that excluded men without property. If the will of the people was in fact to be expressed by voting, it was important that each vote be independent and uncoerced. But a man who had no property and who was dependent on his landlord or employer for survival was thought to be too vulnerable to pressure. It was feared that if such men voted, the result would not be the will of all individuals, for landlords and employers could in effect exercise multiple votes.

Married women were seen to be in much the same situation as unpropertied men. In accordance with antique British tradition, when a woman married, her civil identity was absorbed by her husband. A married couple became a legal fiction; like a corporation, the pair was a single person with a single will. The fictional volition of the pair was always taken to be the same as the actual will of the husband. Husband and wife were, it was sometimes said, "one person" at law. Because they shared a single will, they could not testify against each other. All property which the wife brought to the marriage was vested in her husband, who could make decisions about it—sell it, rent it out, or alter it radically—without her consent.

It is important to note that there were *some* constraints on what the husband might do. For example, widows had the right to *dower*—that is, to the use of one-third of the land which their husband had owned. If the husband proposed to sell any lands which might cut into the dower, the wife had to give her separate consent to a deed of sale, which she signed alone before a judge. This private examination was supposed to offer some protection against duress, but it could not have offered much since the woman returned to *coverture* afterwards. Judges thought it was unwholesome for husband and wife to have separate economic interests; "it relaxes the great bond of family union," said one South Carolina judge.

If a married woman could not buy and sell property without her husband's consent—if she was in fact "covered" by her husband's identity for civil and political (though not criminal) purposes—then it stood to reason that she ought not to vote. To give a vote to a person so dependent on another's will was in fact to give a double vote to the husband, rather than to enfranchise the wife. In a society in which it was assumed that the wife did the husband's bidding, it seemed absurd to give married men a political advantage over their unmarried brothers.

The logic that excluded married women should not have, on the face of it, excluded unmarried women—including widows—who were not under the immediate influence of an adult man and who could buy and sell their property and did pay taxes. Only in New Jersey, where the state constitution of 1776 granted suffrage to "all free inhabitants" who could meet property and residence requirements, did women vote; in 1790, possibly because of Quaker influence, an election law used the phrase "he or she" in referring to voters. The general tendency in suffrage law throughout the nineteenth century was to broaden the electorate by gradually eliminating property and racial qualifications; yet, the New Jersey election statute of 1790 was not replicated elsewhere. Why?

In New Jersey in 1797, women were thought to have voted as a bloc in favor of the Federalist candidate for the state legislature in Elizabethtown. Their votes appeared to have made a real difference in the outcome of the election. In its aftermath, the defeated Democratic-Republicans launched a bitter and snide campaign. The campaign had two themes, which were to appear and reappear as long as women's suffrage was debated in this country: first, that women who appeared at the polls were unfeminine—forgetful of their proper place—and second, that women were easily manipulated—if not by husbands, then by fathers and brothers—so that to enfranchise any woman was in fact to give some man or men undue influence. It took ten years for the campaign to gain its victory, but in 1807 New Jersey passed a new election law excluding all women from the polls, and no other state attempted New Jersey's experiment of 1776.

What did women think of all this? Published commentary by women on their political situation is rare, which is perhaps not surprising when we consider that men virtually controlled the press—pamphlets as well as newspapers. It may be that most women, like most men, took the logic of women's exclusion for granted; it is always hard to regard something as valid in principle which has never actually been practiced. Nevertheless, we can find a few occasions in which women expressed, sometimes bitterly, their belief that they had been unreasonably excluded from the political community. Ironically, one of the most powerful statements is fictional and written by a man. The words that Charles Brockden Brown puts into the mouth of his imaginary heroine, Mrs. Carter, ring with such force that one suspects that he must have heard similar ones in his conversations with the liberal New York women who were his friends and colleagues. "Even the government of our country, which is said to be the freest in the world, passes over women as if they were not. . . . Lawmakers thought as little of comprehending us in their code of liberty, as if we were pigs, or sheep." *(Alcuin: A Dialogue).*

"I have Don as much to Carrey on the Warr as maney that Sett now at ye healm of government. . . ," complained Rachel Wells of Bordentown, New Jersey, who had bought Continental bonds and had to petition (unsuccessfully) for repayment after the war. Although Wells' petition does not mention voting, she does offer a starting point for consideration of women's political role. She knew very well that she had made serious sacrifices for the Revolution: "say of me . . . if She did not fight She threw in all her mite which bought ye Sogers food & Clothing & Let them have Blankets. . . ." Wells felt she had a right to some response.

Abigail Adams suggested that women had an interest in the laws of the new republic, and she explicitly linked the matter of representation to that issue. A Congress which had led a revolution over the issue of "no taxation without representation" certainly could be expected to understand that. It is important to note the *limits* of Abigail Adams' proposals: a close reading of her letters of March 31 and April 27, 1776, will reveal that her primary concern is the vulnerability of women to brutality and abuse from their husbands. "Do not put such unlimited power into the hands of Husbands. Remember all Men would be tyrants if they could. . . ."

What the Constitution did *not* say may have been quite as important as what it did. It usually speaks of "persons"; only rarely does it use the generic "he." Most importantly, the Constitution establishes no voting requirements, leaving it up to the states to set the terms by which people shall qualify to vote.

> **Article I, Section 2:** The House of Representatives shall be composed of Members chosen every second Year by the People of the several States, and the Electors in each State shall have the Qualifications requisite for Electors of the most numerous Branch of the State Legislature.

Thus, women were not explicitly excluded from voting or from membership in Congress. Indeed, the Constitution left an astonishing number of substantive matters open to change, either by amendment or state option. This flexibility is an important reason for the resilience of the American Constitution, and helps to explain its survival when other, more detailed republican constitutions of the era, like the French, were replaced within a generation. The way was left open for individual states to admit women to suffrage, as some indeed did well before the federal amendment. The way was left open for women to be absorbed fully into the political community. Not until *Minor v. Happerset* did the Supreme Court rule that this must happen as a result of explicit legislation, rather than by interpretation of the implication of the Constitution.

In 1876, at the centennial celebration of independence, feminists held a counter-centennial, at which Susan B. Anthony delivered an oration calling for the impeachment of the officers of government on the grounds that they had been false to the principles of the Declaration of Independence and to some of the requirements of the Constitution. She specifically referred to the taxation of women without representation and to the fact that since women could not serve on juries, female defendants were denied a trial by a jury of their peers. The division of the community into a class of men, which governed, and a class of women, which was governed, was, she said, "incompatible with the first principles of freedom." She ended with this ringing conclusion:

> And now, at the close of a hundred years, as the hour-hand of the great clock that marks the centuries points to 1876, we declare our faith in the principles of self-government; our full equality with man in natural rights; that woman was made first for her own happiness, with the absolute right to herself—to all the opportunities and advantages life affords for her complete development; and we

deny that dogma of the centuries, incorporated in the codes of all nations—that woman was made for man—her best interests, in all cases, to be sacrificed to his will. We ask of our rulers, at this hour, no special privileges, no special legislation. We ask justice, we ask equality, we ask that all the civil and political rights that belong to citizens of the United States, be guaranteed to us and our daughters forever.

TEACHING ACTIVITIES

A Do-It-Yourself Constitution

Denny L. Schillings

Introduction

This activity is meant to be used *before* formal study of the Constitution. Its purpose is to induce students to think about the difficulties associated with the creation of the United States Constitution. For students who have studied the Constitution in other classes, the activity can be a recall exercise, as well as a creative one. How accurate the final product is, or how great the students' recall, is not the issue, however. By working through the activity, students will become acquainted with the difficulties, decisions, and compromises that were involved in writing the Constitution.

The activity may seem to be incompletely developed, in that it does not provide detailed choices or questions. This is by design. Its purpose is to stimulate students to study specific contents of the Constitution. That goal having been accomplished, teachers and students should be in a good position to examine the historical specifics together.

This activity is intended for all secondary grades. Teachers will find students' work to be of surprisingly similar quality at all levels. The major difference will be in the level of understanding of the complexity and difficulty of writing a constitution. (Accelerated groups will tend to be more analytical than others.)

Procedure

Before formal study of the Constitution:

1. Distribute "From the Framers to You: A Do-It-Yourself Constitution" and "Problems and Pointers"—the two resource sheets for this activity.
2. Explain to the students that they are going to write a constitution. Encourage them by explaining that all answers will be equally acceptable, as long as they are offered seriously and can be defended rationally.
3. Allow the students time to read through the resource sheets and ask questions.
4. Make a homework assignment for each student to go through the activity and answer the questions. (Students should not spend a great deal of time in writing detailed answers. The only purpose of the assignment is to make them familiar with the materials.)
5. Divide the class into groups of three or five. (Groups should have odd numbers, so that there can be a "majority" opinion in decisions.) Tell them that they will be working together the next day to create a constitution.
6. On the day of the activity, arrange the desks into the assigned groups, and review the purpose of the activity.
7. Inform the students that in order to include something in their constitution, a majority of their group must agree to it. Direct them to choose one group

member to record their discussions. Tell students the maximum time they will have to work on the activity. (The design is for one class-period; however, classes can be given additional time as necessary to accommodate lively debates and discussions.)

8. Begin the activity, and do not be discouraged if things get off to a slow start—the tempo will increase.
9. At the end of the allotted time, each group should hand in its constitution. (This is simply to force groups to finish.)
10. As a follow-up to the activity (probably on the next day), write the four categories from item C of the first resource sheet on the chalkboard. Solicit information for each. (Be sure to involve each group in telling its solutions. *Do not let any one group dominate the discussion.*) Reemphasize to students that their answers are not wrong, so long as they can defend their reasons for giving them.
11. In the process of writing a "constitution" on the board, be sure to ask students *why* they decided as they did. (This is very important, because each group should hear the difficulties encountered and the reasoning employed by other groups.) Teachers should allow an entire class-period to complete steps 10 and 11.
12. When the process of writing down and discussing the students' answers is completed, actual study of the Constitution should begin at the earliest opportunity.

FROM THE FRAMERS TO YOU: A DO-IT-YOURSELF CONSTITUTION

A. Situation

You are a delegate to the Constitutional Convention meeting in Philadelphia in 1787. You have come to solve some of the problems that have arisen since the Articles of Confederation went into effect.

After several days of debate, the convention has decided that a totally new constitution, rather than an amended Articles of Confederation, is needed. It has also decided that a three-part government (one with executive, legislative, and judicial branches) will be used.

Remember, as you are deciding what will go into the basic structure, you are making a government for a nation of many kinds of people: rural and urban, rich and poor, day laborers and professionals. Compromise is essential! Be brief in your solutions, but be thorough. You want this government to survive and prosper. It can do that only if the constitution is workable.

B. Problem

You are to design a new constitution. Be specific about how it will operate and the powers it will have. You should use the following series of questions, listed under four headings, to assist you in addressing the most pressing concerns in creating the government.

C. Questions to be dealt with in writing the constitution

1. Legislative Branch
   a. What kind of duties should legislators be responsible for in the government?

b. How many divisions (houses) should the legislative branch have?
c. What requirements must a person meet to be elected to the legislature? (age, residency, citizenship, sex, etc.)
d. How will legislators be chosen?
e. How long should they serve? More than one term? How many terms?

2. Executive Branch
   a. What kinds of duties should members of the executive branch be responsible for in the government?
   b. What requirements will a person need to meet to be elected president or vice president? (age, citizenship, place of birth, sex, etc.)
   c. How will the president and vice president be chosen?
   d. How long should they serve? Can they be re-elected? If so, how many times?
   e. Will it be possible to remove these people from office? If so, for what reasons? Who would remove them?
3. Judicial Branch
   a. Why does the government need a system of national courts?
   b. What kinds of cases will the national courts decide? How much authority will they have?
   c. How will the judges be chosen? For terms of what duration?
   d. Should the independence of the courts be protected?
4. Other
   a. Will it be possible at a later time to change your constitution? How?
   b. Will your constitution allow new states to join your union? How?
   c. Are there any other things the constitution should provide for, that do not fall specifically under one of the three branches? If so, what are they?

PROBLEMS AND POINTERS

When dealing with the questions of duties and responsibilities, you may want to use all, some, or none of the suggestions listed below. You may, of course, want to assign other duties and responsibilities not listed here. Add them as you wish. You will need to decide which branch of the government (if any) should be responsible for items that you add.

Who should have the power to:

1. make laws?
2. determine the grounds upon which someone may be removed from office?
3. keep a bill from becoming a law (veto)?
4. override a veto?
5. borrow money?
6. collect taxes?
7. regulate commerce?
8. determine the value of money?
9. establish a postal system?
10. declare war?
11. raise and support an army and navy?
12. command the armed forces?
13. grant reprieves and pardons?
14. negotiate and adopt treaties?
15. appoint ambassadors and judges of the Supreme Court?
16. decide if laws meet the intent of the constitution?

17. resolve disputes between states?
18. resolve disputes between a state and citizens of another state?
19. resolve conflicts between state and federal laws?
20. determine if there are some things that a state cannot do? (What?)
21. define treason?
22. decide what obligations states should have toward each other?
23. guarantee that people of all religions—or no religion—have a right to hold office?
24. approve of your constitution to enable it to go into effect?

DISTINGUISHING FEDERALIST AND ANTI-FEDERALIST IDEAS

James A. Duea

Introduction

This activity is intended to teach students to distinguish between Federalist and Anti-federalist principles. It employs two resource sheets to assist them in mastering the distinction. The first is a chart identifying opposed tenets of Federalist and Anti-federalist philosophies of government. The second is an account of the actions and positions taken by an anonymous, "mystery" delegate to the Constitutional Convention in Philadelphia in 1787. Without knowing that this account logs the actual speeches, motions, and votes of a real delegate—Luther Martin, an Anti-federalist from the state of Maryland—students will be asked to determine whether each action or position in the account reflects Federalist or Anti-federalist thinking.

Luther Martin (1744–1826) made a great imprint upon the history of the United States; yet, his name is often omitted or given little attention in history books. The obscurity of Luther Martin is undoubtedly related to the parts he played in our early history. He was the unofficial spokesman of the Anti-federalists at the Constitutional Convention, refused to sign the Constitution of 1787, fought for its defeat during the ratification process in his home state of Maryland, became a personal adversary of Thomas Jefferson, represented Aaron Burr at his trial for treason, and represented the state of Maryland in the memorable case involving the U.S. Bank. In all of these roles, he appears as an individual who was opposed to the principles upon which this country was founded, and therefore his name is fading from history.

It is not the primary purpose of this project to revive his memory, but rather, through an examination of his role in the political struggle which produced the Constitution of 1787, to provide students with a more thorough understanding of the document and its development.

Procedure

1. Before beginning the activity, guide students in reading the Constitution.
2. Discuss the differences in Federalist and Anti-federalist perspectives, distributing the resource sheet, "Federalist vs. Anti-federalist Principles," to assist in the discussion.
3. Distribute the account of the actions of the "mystery" delegate to the Constitutional Convention.
4. Ask students to read the account. For each date, the student should label the action "F" (if it appears to reflect Federalist thinking), "A" (if it appears to reflect Anti-federalist thinking), or "U" (if the student is uncertain or feels that the action reflects neither Federalist nor Anti-federalist thinking).
5. Divide the class into groups of three or four students, and direct them to reach a consensus on each action.

6. Ask the groups to arrive at conclusions in the following matters:
   - Was this delegate a Federalist or an Anti-federalist? (What makes you think so?)
   - Was he one of the 39 delegates who signed the document, or one of the 16 who declined to sign?
7. Re-form the class into a single group, and share results. The concluding discussion should also cover:
   - Contributions of Anti-federalists to the final document.
   - The importance of compromise.
   - Speculation as to why this delegate did not sign.

PRINCIPLES AND BELIEFS	
FEDERALISM	**ANTI-FEDERALISM**
National sovereignty (consolidation of power in a *strong national government*)	State sovereignty (preservation of states' rights in *strong state governments*)
Republicanism can flourish in a large political entity	Republicanism can exist only in small political entities
States should be represented in the national government according to their populations	All states should have an equal voice in the national government
Strong executive	Strong legislature (particularly lower house)
Rule by few or elite; indirect selection of officials acceptable	Rule by many; officials directly elected by the people
Bill of rights unnecessary to a constitution	Bill of rights essential for preserving individual liberties
Long terms of office; unlimited number of terms	Short terms of office (annual elections); limited number of terms

A BRIEF ACCOUNT OF THE MAJOR SPEECHES, MOTIONS, AND VOTES OF ______, DELEGATE TO THE CONSTITUTIONAL CONVENTION, PHILADELPHIA 1787

June 9 —Took his seat as a delegate from __________.

June 11 —Moved that state officers should not have to take an oath of allegiance to the new Constitution. Indicated that the state oaths are sufficient.

June 21 —Seconded a motion: "that the first branch (House of Representatives), instead of being elected by the people, should be elected in such a manner as the Legislature of each State should direct."

June 27 —Spoke at length as to why each state should be represented equally in the House of Representatives.

June 28 —Stated that the general (national) government should be formed for the states, not for individuals. He also spoke in favor of each state having an equal number of votes in Congress.

July 2 —Voted in favor of the following motion: "Resolved that in the second branch of the Legislature of the United States (Senate), each state shall have an equal vote."

July 14 —Stated that if representation in the House of Representatives is to be based on population, the other house should be based on the principle of equality.

July 16 —Voted in favor of the Connecticut Compromise.

July 17 —Spoke against a resolution that would permit the national legislature to veto laws passed by the state legislatures.

July 17 —Made the following motion: "That the legislative acts of the United States, made by virtue and in pursuance of the Articles of Union, and all treaties made and ratified under the authority of the United States, shall be the Supreme Law of the respective States, as far as these acts or treaties shall relate to the said States, or their citizens and inhabitants; and that the judiciary of the several States shall be bound thereby in their decisions, anything in the respective laws of the individual states to the contrary notwithstanding."

July 17 —Moved regarding the executive: "The Executive be chosen by Electors appointed by the several legislatures of the individual States."

July 17 —Spoke strenuously for the judges to be appointed by the Senate.

July 18 —Stated that the suppression of insurrections should be a responsibility of the states.

July 19 —Moved during the debate on limiting the terms of the President, that the following words should be inserted: "to be ineligible a second time."

July 19 —Voted in favor of a six-year term for the President.

July 20 —Voted in favor of the President being removed from office through impeachment by the Congress.

July 23 —Spoke against the representation in the Senate based upon population.

July 24 —Made the following motion: "that the appointment of the executive shall continue for eleven years."

August 6 —Spoke against a bicameral legislature and the people electing representatives to the Congress.

August 13—Spoke in favor of the state legislatures ratifying the Constitution.

August 14—Stated that since the Senate is to represent the states, the members of it ought to be paid by the states.

August 17—Stated that the consent of the state should precede the introduction of outside forces to put down a rebellion in the state.

August 18—Moved that the army in time of peace should be limited by the Constitution.

August 20—Proposed that "no act or acts done by one or more of the States against the United States, or by any citizen of any one of the United States, under the authority of one or more of the said States, shall be deemed treason, or punished as such; but in case of war being levied by one or more of the States against the United States, the conduct of each party towards the other, and their adherents respectively, shall be regulated by the laws of war and of nations."

August 21—Proposed that the importation of slaves should not be permitted.

August 21—Made a motion that if direct taxes are necessary, the states should determine the mode of taxation in their respective states.

August 27—Voted in favor of the motion giving the executive command of the militia, so as to read: "and if the militia of the several States, when called into the actual service of the United States."

August 29—Seconded the motion: "That no act of the legislature for the purpose of regulating the commerce of the United States with foreign powers, among the several States shall be passed without the assent of two-thirds of the members of each House."

August 30—Moved that: "New States may be admitted by the Legislature (Congress) into the union; but no new State shall be hereafter formed or created within the jurisdiction of any of the present States without the consent of the legislature of such State, as well as the general Legislature (Congress).

August 31—Insisted that the legislatures of the States ratify the new Constitution.

BLACK PEOPLE AND THE CONSTITUTION

Bonny M. Cochran and Linda K. Kerber

Introduction

This activity asks students to read the Constitution carefully and then consider a few other contemporary documents. The task that students are directed to undertake requires them to give special attention to the treatment of slavery in the Constitution. Students are asked to decide whether the Constitution could originally be seen as protecting "life, liberty, and the pursuit of happiness" for black people.

Procedure

1. Assist students in reviewing what the Constitution says or implies about slavery: the three-fifths compromise (Article 1, Section 2); the slave trade (Article II, Section 9); and fugitive slaves (Article IV, Section 2). Students should also review sections in their textbooks dealing with the constitutional compromises over slavery.
2. Divide the class into groups of four or five. Explain that the task of each group is to decide what a black family in 1833 should do when one of its members has been given her freedom. (Further instructions are provided in the resource sheet, "Setting the Stage.")
3. Direct each group to read "Setting the Stage" and consider the hypothetical options it presents for the Jackson family.
4. Ask each group to complete the second resource sheet, "Group Decision Report," to turn in to the teacher.
5. To conclude the activity, ask students the following questions in full-class discussion:
   - Where did your group decide that the Jacksons should go?
   - What additional information would you like to have in order to confirm your decision?
   - What additional advantages and disadvantages did your group see in each option?
   - How do the circumstances faced by the Jackson family differ from the circumstances faced by a minority family today?
   - What was difficult about this activity? What was easy?

SETTING THE STAGE

Upon the death of her owner, Amelia Jackson (age 24) has been freed. Her husband, Marcus, is still a slave on a neighboring plantation. They have one child—Betty (age 7). (Two other children died in infancy.) The year is 1833. They live about ten miles outside of Richmond, Virginia. They have no debts, and Marcus has managed to save a little money from extra work as a carpenter.

The Jacksons are descended from Africans who were brought to Virginia in 1690. They have many relatives in the Richmond area, most of whom live as slaves on other plantations.

According to Virginia law of 1806, all freed slaves must leave the state within six months to avoid setting an example which would make other slaves envious and perhaps rebellious. Amelia Jackson must decide what she will do. Although Betty is still a slave, Amelia could try to take her daughter with her. Marcus Jackson is willing to try to escape with them; he feels he has a good chance of getting away.

What should they do?

OPTION A—RICHMOND, VIRGINIA

Advantages: They would stay in an area which is familiar to them. Only one of them would be breaking the law. Amelia would have to hide in Richmond, visiting her daughter on one plantation and her husband on another. They would be close to their relatives, who mean a lot to them.

Disadvantages: Marcus and Betty would still be slaves. The family would be living in three separate locations. If Amelia were caught, she could be sold into slavery.

OPTION B—BOSTON, MASSACHUSETTS

During the Revolution, the state of Massachusetts adopted a new state constitution. It began with the words, "All men are born free and equal, and have certain natural, essential, and unalienable rights; among which may be reckoned the right of enjoying . . . their . . . liberties." In a few years after 1780, slavery withered away in Massachusetts. Some slaves simply left their masters. Some masters assumed that the state constitution required them to regard their former slaves as free.

In the spring of 1781, a court made it official. A man named Quock Walker (or Quark: the translation from the original African language is not exact) ran away from his owner, claiming that his master's wife, now dead, had promised him his freedom when he reached twenty-one. Walker's master, Nathaniel Jennison, beat him and tried to force him back to work. But Walker was helped by the relatives of his dead mistress to appeal to the Supreme Judicial Court of Massachusetts. A promise made to a slave would not stand up in Court. But the Chief Justice ruled that "the idea of slavery is inconsistent with our [state] constitution; and there can be no such thing as perpetual servitude of a rational creature, unless his liberty is forfeited by some criminal conduct or given up by personal consent or contract. . . . Slavery is in my judgement as effectively abolished as it can be."

Advantages: In the years after 1781, the free black population of Massachusetts grew. If the Jackson family had come to Boston in 1830, they would have found 1,875 other free blacks there. Free blacks made up three percent of the total population of the city. In 1831, William Lloyd Garrison began editing the first major anti-slavery newspaper, *The Liberator,* in Boston. The Jacksons would find that there were groups of people organized in anti-slavery societies to lobby against slavery. They would also find some small businesses owned by black people. There had been a small school for black children since 1798, and a very high proportion of black people in Boston could read and write.

The state constitution had long been understood to outlaw slavery in Massachusetts.

Disadvantages: The Jacksons would find that most blacks lived in certain neighborhoods. (These were not formally segregated; some whites lived in them, too. But black people were concentrated in certain of the poorest areas.) Virtually no black people owned their own homes. The vast majority of black people were unskilled laborers and servants, working in marginal jobs. Many public accommodations were segregated. Schools were segregated (until 1855). Marcus's and Betty's masters might take advantage of the fugitive slave clause.

OPTION C—NEW YORK CITY

New York did not outlaw slavery until nineteen years after the Constitution of the state of Massachusetts was framed. In 1799, New York passed a *gradual* manumission law. It provided that male children born to slaves after July 4, 1799, would be free when they reached the age of twenty-eight, and female children, after the age of twenty-five. If the Jacksons came to New York in 1830, they would have found more than 12,000 black people there, but some of them were still slaves.

Advantages: New York had a much larger black community than Boston; there were over 10,000 blacks there in 1820. It would be easier for Marcus to hide among them if his master tried to track him down. There were more possibilities for employment for black workers in New York. A significant proportion of free black men found employment as mariners on ships using the port of New York. Other men and women found work in retailing, as bakers, grocers, peddlers, and carters, as well as in domestic service. There were several institutions established by black people: two black churches, two free black schools, and an aid society—the New York African Society for Mutual Relief.

Disadvantages: Because slavery had been abolished more recently and more gradually than in Massachusetts, more white people still thought that slavery was the "natural" position for blacks. In fact, as late as 1790, New York had been second only to Charleston, South Carolina, in the number of slaves in the city. There was probably more racism and more hostility to blacks in New York than in Boston. There would be a great deal of segregation—in churches, in public transportation. There were few good schools which would accept black children, and schools in New York would not be desegregated when Boston schools were in 1855. Betty's and Marcus's masters could invoke the fugitive slave clause and search for them in New York.

OPTION D—CANADA

Upper Canada, including what is now Ontario, was settled heavily by Loyalists who had fled the American Revolution and brought their slaves with them. In 1793, the Canadian Parliament passed a gradual emancipating law which freed all children born to slaves when they reached their twenty-fifth birthday. The law also provided that "No Negro or other person who shall come or be brought into this Province . . . shall be subject to the condition of a slave or to . . . involuntary service for life." In 1833, a British court ruled that no slavery could exist in any part of the British Empire, thus abolishing slavery completely in Canada.

Advantages: If the Jacksons were to go to Canada, Betty and Marcus would be legally free. Marcus Jackson could fight in the militia. They would find sizeable communities of runaway slaves and former slaves who had been freed by Canadian law. Their masters would not be able to pursue them, because the provisions of the fugitive slave clause would not be recognized in a foreign country.

Disadvantages: They would be very far from their relatives, with virtually no chance of seeing them again. Most black people in Canada lived in small settlements. They were very poor, and there were few economic opportunities.

Question: If the Jacksons were to go to Canada, they would have to change their allegiance from the United States to Canada. Would they regard this as an advantage or a disadvantage?

GROUP DECISION REPORT: WHAT SHOULD THE JACKSONS DO?

Names of students in this group:

Discuss the options that are theoretically possible for the Jacksons and then list—from best to worst—choices that you would advise them to make. Be prepared to explain why you ranked the choices as you did.

We recommend that the Jackson family make plans to carry out these choices, in this order of preference, and here are our reasons:

Best choice, and reasons:

Second best choice, and reasons:

Third best choice, and reasons:

Worst choice, and reasons:

THE PATH TO POLITICAL POWER FOR WOMEN

Bonny M. Cochran

Introduction

This activity presents the fictional quest of Maria Grander to win political office in the United States today. It provides a variety of opportunities for studying the Constitution at different levels of complexity. It compels students to examine the Constitution closely, learning and applying the specific procedures and requirements for seeking and holding national political office. Students are called upon to answer practical questions posed by a young woman anxious to begin a political career as a legislator. The process of discovering what the Constitution says—and fails to say—in response to Maria's questions can motivate students to examine the reasons for particular constitutional provisions. This process will engage students in an investigation of the intentions of the framers and the changes that Americans of different identities have experienced since 1787.

Procedure

1. Distribute the resource sheet, "Path to Political Power: Maria Grander's Campaign," to all students and ask them to read it, answering the questions at each **STOP.** *Or,* alternatively, divide the class into four or five groups (five, if you decide to ask one group to work on the optional questions under **STOP E**) and assign one **STOP** to each group.
2. Ask students (or groups) to report their answers, and discuss them.
3. Formalize the students' responses under the headings *Custom, Constitution,* and *Important for Women* on the chalkboard. Ask students to suggest items for each heading.

PATH TO POLITICAL POWER: MARIA GRANDER'S CAMPAIGN

Read the short fictional sketch about Maria Grander below. At each STOP, refer to the Constitution, including the Amendments, in your textbook, and answer the questions. The questions at each STOP refer to the paragraph immediately preceding.

Maria had not been interested in politics until seven years ago. Now here she was, in her home town of LeMoyne, Iowa, celebrating her 27th birthday with her close friends. Not only were all of the people at the party interested in politics, but all were also actively involved. In fact, two of them held elected political offices and the rest of the dozen people there had worked in political campaigns to help elect candidates they supported and to win approval of or to defeat referendum questions they considered important. After the "Happy Birthday" song and congratulations, conversation turned to Maria's plans.

"I think you should run to represent our district in the House of Representatives," said Fred. "Yes, I'd really like to do that," responded Maria, "but even though I work in and am active in this district, don't forget I have always lived across the county line, in the next district." She went on to remember that her family had lived in the same neighborhood ever since they had all moved here from Mexico, when she had been a baby. (The family all had become naturalized citizens of the U.S. as soon as possible.) "Don't you think I would have to live in the district which I want to represent?" she asked. "It might be smart, but I don't know if you have to," was the reply.

STOP A

1. According to the Constitution, does Maria meet the legal requirements to be a member of the House of Representatives?
   - age
   - residence
   - citizenship
2. Is there any other national office for which Maria is eligible? Why?
3. Looking to the future, are there offices for which she will become eligible? Are there offices for which she will never be eligible? Why?

The conversation went on. "Do you think it will be hard for Maria to get elected because she's a woman?", her college roommate, Suzanne, asked. "Not any harder than for a young man with a similar record," answered Jorge, "but we should start thinking about how she can win the Democratic Party primary and get the nomination. After we do that, we can think about how tough it will be to beat the incumbent Republican in November."

STOP B

1. What does the Constitution say about political parties and primary elections?
2. Write a short definition of *incumbent,* and then list some reasons an incumbent usually has an advantage in getting elected.

"Oh, it should be easy for Maria; the party leaders will support her. She will help balance the ticket in two ways—with the women's vote and the Hispanic vote. Lots of people will identify with her and see her as being able to represent their interests," commented Robert. "Let's not make that assumption too fast; traditions die hard here. You know our state has never been represented by a woman in Congress," Maria pointed out. "Yes, but that's not as bad as the state where my cousins live," Tony chimed in. "There, a law says that no married woman can hold a state job if her husband is employed by the state—that sure would end these plans—or the plans for Maria's wedding next month, since Walter [Maria's fiancé] teaches at the state university." Maria said that living in another district was bad enough and that she was glad they were not living where Tony's cousins live.

STOP C

1. What does the Constitution say about these characteristics for any elected office?
   - sex
   - marital status
2. What does the Constitution say about the supremacy of the U.S. Constitution over state laws and constitutions? What does that imply about the law for married women?

3. Do you find anything in the Constitution which would indicate a concern on the part of the framers that *all* groups of people in the population should be represented?
4. If Maria had been making her plans before 1920, would her ability to draw the "women's vote" have been of any help to her? (*Hint:* Check Article I, Section 2, paragraph a, and then Amendment 19.)

Maria went home and discussed her plans with her parents. Although her father was not enthusiastic about the effort, he offered some strategic advice. "You are so young. It's better now for young people; at least they can vote sooner. Let's hope they will vote for you. You'd better go around and make sure that all of the people have registered and paid their poll taxes in time."

STOP D
1. What change in voter qualifications was Maria's father referring to?
2. Was Maria's father right in advising her to make sure that everyone had paid his or her poll tax? Why, or why not?

Maria did gather political support, enter the primary and gain her party's nomination to run against the opposition party in the general election. During the campaign she encountered other problems: whether she was guaranteed equal time in the media for campaigning, whether she had the right to distribute campaign literature inside a bar, and so forth. The election will take place next week. Everyone awaits the outcome.

STOP E (optional)
1. Continue the story, inventing other situations a candidate could face which would be answered by referring to the Constitution or to a Supreme Court decision applying or interpreting the Constitution.
2. Ask other people—students not in this class or adults—to read Maria's story and then interview them on their opinions of the likelihood of Maria's success.

THE CONSTITUTION DECODED: A SHOPPER'S GUIDE TO THE TEXT*

John W. Larner

Introduction

This activity provides students with an overview of the contents and arrangement of the original body of the United States Constitution. It equips them with a device for remembering where specific information is located. The subjects addressed in each of the seven articles are easily mastered when students memorize this associational sentence: **Lazy elephants jump slowly and sit regularly.**

This is how the sentence works:

Word	Article	Topic
Lazy	I	**L**egislative branch; distribution of powers
Elephants	II	**E**xecutive branch
Jump	III	**J**udicial branch
Slowly	IV	**S**tates and territories—guarantees and responsibilities
And	V	**A**mending the Constitution
Sit	VI	**S**upremacy of the federal Constitution, laws, and treaties
Regularly	VII	**R**atification of the Constitution

Procedure

Explain to students that the original document of the Constitution opens with a Preamble which lists reasons for writing it. Then point out that the original body of the Constitution is divided into seven Articles dealing with distinct topics. (At this stage, a short review of Roman numerals is sometimes appropriate.) Introduce the associational sentence and demonstrate its usefulness. Having committed it to memory, students will be ready for the following exercise.

WHERE IN THE UNITED STATES CONSTITUTION?

Where in the body of the original United States Constitution would information about each of the following topics be found? Write the correct article numbers in the proper blanks, using Roman numerals. Add the columns, expressing each

---

*Adapted and reprinted with permission of the Pennsylvania Department of Education, from *Pennsylvania and Constitutional Development 1776–1794: A Lesson Packet for Secondary Schools,* prepared by John Larner (James Wetzler, Social Studies Adviser).

sum as an Arabic number. You should come up with the year of the Constitutional Convention in Philadelphia. Then answer the last question. By adding that number to the convention date, you should get the year in which the United States Constitution took effect.

In which article of the United States Constitution would you find information about. . .

Organization of Congress? —
Supremacy of federal law over state law? —
Powers of Congress? —
How to amend the Constitution? —
Responsibilities of the states? —
Qualifications of members of Congress? —
Powers of the federal courts? —
Approval of the Constitution? —
Territories? —
Year of the Philadelphia Constitutional Convention? — — — —
Qualifications for the Presidency? —
Year the United States Constitution took effect? — — — —

Part II

The Nineteenth Century

CHAPTER 3

INTERPRETING AND AMENDING THE CONSTITUTION

Herman Belz

A constitution is the complex of principles, institutions, laws, practices, and traditions by which a people organize and conduct their political and governmental life. The purpose of the United States Constitution, as of Western constitutions in general, is to establish, or constitute, the governmental power necessary to maintain social order and stability, while at the same time imposing limits on government in order to protect individual liberty and social freedom.

A constitution may take the form of a written charter of government, supplemented by organic statutes and institutional practices, as in the United States, or it may be embodied in documents, laws, customs, and institutions of diverse historical provenance, as in England. In either case, it seeks to place beyond political dispute basic decisions concerning the fundamental values and goals of the society, the rights and responsibilities of individual citizens, and the organization and legitimate exercise of governmental power. Moreover, whether written or unwritten, a constitution achieves its principal effect through the internalization in individual citizens of the values, rules, and procedures that it prescribes for the conduct of public life.

The framers of the United States Constitution gave it form as a set of prescriptive requirements that were declared to be the supreme law of the land and that were regarded as enforceable in practice in ordinary courts of law. Accordingly, although its meaning was fixed and theoretically unalterable except through the process of amendment specified in the document itself, the Constitution could, like all law, be interpreted by those whose actions it prescribed. The principal governmental actors charged with maintaining the Constitution—and in effect with interpreting and applying it—were the officers of the three separate branches of government—the legislature, the executive, and the judiciary.

In the nineteenth century, the judiciary, in the famous case of *Marbury v. Madison* (1803), staked an early claim to the duty of saying what the Constitution meant. This was in keeping with the traditional Anglo-American view that it was the special function of courts to discover or declare the meaning of the law. Throughout the nineteenth century, however, the power of judicial review was exercised sparingly at the federal level.

Moreover, constitutional interpretation and the settlement of constitutional controversies were far from being the exclusive preserve of the courts. Sometimes, as in the conflict aroused by the Alien and Sedition Acts in 1798, or the protective tariff in 1832, the states themselves attempted to settle the meaning of the Constitution. Less dramatically perhaps, but more decisively, lawmakers and executive officers, in exercising the powers assigned to them, interpreted the meaning of critical constitutional provisions. Constitutional interpretation in the nineteenth century may thus be understood as proceeding along two interrelated courses. The judicial branch explicated sections of constitutional law, while the legislative and executive branches shaped strategies of constitutional politics and agendas for public policy.

Speaking most frequently and authoritatively through Chief Justice John Marshall, the Supreme Court in the first third of the nineteenth century laid down the basic doctrines of American constitutional law. The Court decided that states could not operate their judicial systems independently of federal authority. It protected private property against legislative interference by insisting on the sanctity of contracts and interpreting the contract clause of the Constitution broadly, as a limitation on state legislative action designed to stimulate private entrepreneurial activity. The Court defined interstate commerce and the power of Congress to regulate commerce among the states in such a way as to encourage national integration. It declared that the federal government was a sovereign nation-state which in the exercise of its constitutional powers could rightfully control all individuals or governments within its territory.

Protected by its equal and coordinate status under the separation of powers, the Supreme Court defined its role in the early national period as that of maintaining constitutional limitations and the rule of law. The Court adhered to a judicial philosophy and employed decisional techniques that, while possessing legal integrity, were broadly responsive to the political temper and sensibilities of republican society.

Andrew Jackson appointed Roger B. Taney to succeed John Marshall as chief justice of the Supreme Court. Under the leadership of Taney, the Court continued to fashion politically responsive rules of constitutional law. Without repudiating the central principles of constitutional interpretation set forth in the Marshall era, the Court under Taney allowed the states more leeway in regulating interstate commerce, contracts, corporations, and economic development in general. Of more immediate political importance, the Taney Court clarified and extended state power over the all-absorbing issue of slavery, eventually deciding in the *Dred Scott* case that the South's peculiar local institution must be regarded as having legal status and enjoying legal protections anywhere in the nation.

By 1860, the Supreme Court's interpretation of federalism as a doctrine of reciprocally and exclusively limited spheres of federal and state power—the theory of dual federalism that drew inspiration from the Tenth Amendment as a kind of supremacy clause for the states—encouraged defenders of slavery categorically to deny federal sovereignty. At that point, it was but a short step to the dissolution of the Union through the ultimate act of state sovereignty—secession.

Secession climaxed decades of controversy over the fundamental question of the nature of the Union—an issue that was eventually settled by political and military means during the Civil War. This fact serves to remind us that, while Congress and the president do not adjudicate controversies at constitutional law, they do make basic constitutional decisions.

In the first critical years of constitutional development, lawmakers and executives decided that:

1. The presidency would be a unitary rather than a multimember or collegial institution.
2. Congress would be in fact as well as in theory a self-starting and self-directing institution, capable of controlling the executive and governing the country.
3. Legislative power would be sovereign in respect to the purposes assigned by the Constitution and would not be confined to expressly enumerated powers.

Congressional legislation providing for a national bank, a protective tariff, the distribution of public lands, an internal transportation and communication system, and the acquisition and government of new territories not only established public policies of great practical importance, but also stood as authoritative determinations of the meaning of the Constitution. Occasionally, a Supreme Court decision might confirm the constitutional validity of legislative action—as in *McCulloch v. Maryland*—but most of the time acts of Congress needed no such judicial approbation.

In the process of promoting policies of national integration and thus defining the scope of federal power, lawmakers and executives altered the constitutional system in a most significant way—they created a system of political parties. To the framers of the Constitution, permanent organized opposition to the government was potentially, if not by definition, treasonous. Yet, the exigencies of adopting public policies under the new constitution spurred the formation of leadership groups at the center of the government espousing rival programs. These competing groups soon stimulated, and were in turn sustained by, political action at the local level.

While superficially divisive, the national two-party system that existed by 1840 actually functioned to integrate sections and interests across the country. Moreover, it operated efficiently in recruiting government officials, managing elections, organizing public opinion, and harmonizing the separate branches of government. Political parties fulfilled the constitutional purpose of a representative institution mediating between the people and the government. And because parties often employed constitutional rhetoric and argumentation, they had the effect of internalizing constitutional values and procedures among the citizenry.

Within a flexible constitutional consensus, political parties functioned as nationalizing institutions. Competing coalitions of interests were permitted to use centralizing or decentralizing conceptions of federalism to promote their different purposes. In the years after 1840, however, deepening and widening conflict over slavery shattered the loose framework of agreement on which constitutional politics had rested. The basic issue in American politics became the place of slavery in a republican society and constitutional order.

In 1860, lawmakers and executives acted through sectionally and ideologically realigned and polarized political parties to insist on their respective versions of political right and constitutional morality. Although constitutionally correct and legal, the election of Abraham Lincoln, a sectional antislavery candidate, so lacked legitimacy in the eyes of a significant minority of southern states that it provoked them to attempt to dissolve the Union by force.

Fighting to maintain the Union and the Constitution, northern lawmakers and executives tried to conduct the struggle in accordance with constitutional rules and procedures. So profound was the nature of the conflict, however, that the means chosen for carrying it on had profound constitutional consequences.

President Lincoln's emergency actions in meeting the Confederate attack on Fort Sumter, together with the subsequent establishment of conscription and internal security systems that restricted individual civil liberty, were forceful and effective interpretations of the Constitution. They defined executive power far more broadly than ever before, and decisively answered the question of whether the government could take extraordinary measures to save both the Union and the Constitution itself. Emancipation of slaves by military means was a similarly decisive exercise of constitutional power that brought far-reaching constitutional changes in its train. For the first time in the history of the republic, the federal government breached the wall of state power that surrounded—and in many instances qualified and restricted—the rights and liberties of individuals.

So important was the abolition of slavery as a national social reform that it was carried out and guaranteed by formal amendment of the Constitution. The amendment process had not been invoked successfully since 1804, when the development of political parties necessitated a change in the method of electing the president and vice-president, embodied in the Twelfth Amendment. Between 1865 and 1870, however, three new amendments were added to the Constitution. Obviously, the Thirteenth, Fourteenth, and Fifteenth Amendments hardly illustrate usual conduct of constitutional politics. It is difficult to conceive of circumstances other than the Civil War in which these reforms could have been adopted.

Nevertheless, these war amendments announced a new birth of freedom and affirmed the equal rights principle as the basis on which national reconciliation must proceed. They contained their own justification as a kind of second founding of the republic. In this sense they were like the original Constitution itself, which had been drafted by the framers and submitted to the states without regard for the constitutional procedures required by the Articles of Confederation.

The Thirteenth Amendment permanently altered federal-state relations and redefined the nature of civil liberty in the United States. It prohibited slavery and nationalized personal liberty, placing it under federal protection against actions of either state governments or private individuals. But this vindication of personal liberty—the preeminent civil right—necessarily implied further restrictions on the power of the states to regulate the civil rights that were inextricably linked with it.

This additional limitation on the states was accomplished by the Fourteenth Amendment, drafted by the Congressional Joint Committee on Reconstruction in 1866 and ratified in 1868. The single most important constitutional change ever adopted, this amendment prohibited the states from depriving persons of life, liberty, and property without due process of law and from denying them equal protection of the laws. Moreover, it gave Congress the power to enforce it by appropriate legislation.

Finally, the Fifteenth Amendment, while allowing suffrage regulation to remain within the jurisdiction of the states, conferred on citizens of the United States the right to vote regardless of race, color, or previous condition of servitude.

Although the full potential of these amendments was not to be realized until the twentieth century, they worked a profound change in the constitutional system. The states still bore the primary responsibility for protecting and regulating civil rights, and the Fourteenth Amendment did not prohibit the denial of civil rights by private individuals. Nevertheless, the federal government had acquired constitutional authority to guarantee personal liberty and individual rights against injurious and discriminatory state action. The language employed to achieve these ends included the unambiguous establishment of paramount national citizenship, something that was not provided in 1787. The assumptions of state sovereignty on which Southerners had tried to erect an impregnable defense of slavery and consign the Negro race to permanent subordination were destroyed. Federal sovereignty, which had long been asserted in policies of national defense and economic development, was now affirmed and exercised to some extent in matters concerning individual civil rights at the local level.

Though deciding the slavery question and the nature of the Union involved limiting state power, nevertheless constitutional decision makers were by no means committed to a total shift of power from the states to the federal government. During and after Reconstruction, states' rights remained a vital constitutional tradition that provided a basis for dealing with social and economic problems caused by the development of national commerce and industry.

State authority in its various forms had long been used to distribute natural resources and promote the productive use of property. This authority included the police power for promoting the health, safety, welfare, and morals of the community; the power of eminent domain; and the common law authority of state courts concerning the affairs of everyday society. When after 1870 the social costs of industrial development began to rival, if not outweigh, the benefits, regulation of the economy became necessary. For this purpose, constitutional innovation was not required so much as the application or extension of traditional doctrines of state power. Accordingly, lawmakers and executives in the states adopted regulatory measures that imposed restrictions on entrepreneurial activity—in particular, railroad corporations and manufacturing and marketing organizations.

Learning from the state experience, federal lawmakers and executives also enacted economic regulatory measures in the late nineteenth century. Congress put the commerce power to new uses in the Interstate Commerce Act of 1887, declaring rules of fair competition in the railroad industry and creating the Interstate Commerce Commission to enforce them. By combining legislative, executive, and judicial powers in a single agency, Congress gave a new interpretation to—if it did not utterly confound—the principle of the separation of powers. This statute anticipated one of the most important constitutional changes of the twentieth century—the rise of the administrative state.

The Sherman Antitrust Act of 1890 was a second regulatory measure based on the commerce power in which Congress nationalized common law rules for restricting monopolistic market practices. Here again, the use made of a traditional federal power for regulatory purposes amounted to a new kind of constitutional interpretation.

In yet another social reform measure, Congress attempted to use the seemingly unassailable federal taxing power to tap the wealth of the new industrial sector of society in the income tax of 1894. The policy behind this statute was considered so threatening to the stability and security of property, however, that the Supreme Court struck it down as unconstitutional in the income tax cases of 1895.

Although these and several other cases show that there were limits to what the judiciary was willing to allow in the way of constitutional innovation in the late nineteenth century, the Supreme Court generally accepted the regulatory activities of the state and federal governments. The traditional deference of the courts to the political branches in matters concerning public policy largely determined this response. Yet, the nineteenth-century judiciary had never been completely passive or indifferent to policy questions—especially issues of economic development. The post-Reconstruction Supreme Court evinced this traditional judicial concern most clearly in its interpretation of the Fourteenth Amendment.

Utilizing the long-established doctrine that a corporation was a legal person, the Supreme Court protected entrepreneurial freedom in a series of rulings that struck down state regulations as unconstitutional deprivations of liberty and property that violated the due process clause of the Fourteenth Amendment. This line of decisions enlarged the sphere of nationally protected civil rights against state interference. In an ironic if unpopular way, it fulfilled one of the basic purposes of the framers of the Civil War constitutional amendments. This assertion of due process also signified a change in the constitutional role of the judiciary. Starting then and continuing without interruption into the twentieth century, courts assumed a larger policy-making function, in which considerations of the reasonableness of legislative or administrative action became the test of its constitutionality.

By 1900, the nation's eighteenth-century Constitution had been significantly altered by formal amendment and legislative, executive, and judicial interpretation. Federalism and the separation of powers remained the organizing principles of constitutional government. The people as constituent power still shaped basic national and state policies through electoral judgments expressed in the actions of the political branches. Yet, the creation of independent regulatory agencies in the national government as well as in the states, and the emergence of a more explicitly policy-oriented and self-consciously political form of judicial review, challenged the traditional dominance of politically representative institutions. These developments augured the wholesale shift to government by the courts and the bureaucracy that would form a major part of constitutional development in the twentieth century.

TEACHING ACTIVITIES

TEACHING THE CONCEPT OF "IMPLIED POWER"

Joseph L. White

Introduction

This activity is designed to allow students to arrive at an understanding of the concept of implied constitutional powers. A dramatic scene, set in a high school social studies class, provides the material for this exercise. Students follow a process of inductive reasoning in a situation which is especially relevant to their daily lives. In the scene, a teacher grants a student permission to get a drink of water, and the student begins to leave the room. But does he have "implied" authority to get out of his seat, open the door, and walk out into the hall? The ensuing debate on this point will serve to clarify the fact that the United States Constitution recognizes both enumerated and implied powers. This understanding will vitally assist students in considering the important case of *Marbury v. Madison.*

Procedure

Teachers can use the classroom drama provided here in a variety of ways. Copies can be distributed for students to read silently or aloud, as a drama. Teachers can assign parts, assuming the role of the teacher themselves and acting out the scene with their students. It might be considerably more effective, however, for teachers simply to take their cue and opening lines from the script, and let an analogous scene unfold in their own classrooms. Teachers who do this might find it useful to control the discussion by stopping the spontaneous classroom performance periodically and referring students to pertinent sections of the script. This tactic might help to clarify the discussion or get it back on track. At these points, students could give dramatic readings of relevant portions of the script and compare their own ideas to those evolved by its characters.

As a follow-up to the activity, the teacher should:

1. Call attention to the similarity of the students' rule in the script for identifying implied powers (those powers which are necessary and reasonable) and the "elastic clause."
2. Ask who should decide whether a certain power is implied. The student? The teacher? Congress? The courts?
3. Define Mary's interpretation of "reasonable" as a *strict interpretation* and Bill's as a *loose interpretation,* and extend the analogy to help students understand the Federalists' and Anti-federalists' positions.
4. Ask students to identify powers that they think may be implied by the enumerated powers.
5. Guide students in considering the case of *Marbury v. Madison.*

YOU CAN LEAD A CLASS TO WATER, BUT CAN YOU MAKE IT THINK?

The setting is a typical high school U.S. History or Government class with one teacher and about 25–30 students. The bell rings. The teacher enters the room after all students have arrived and shuts the door. The teacher sits down at the desk and takes roll. There is quiet talk from the students until the teacher rises and looks around the classroom.

TEACHER: Good morning. Would anyone like to get a drink of water?

[At first there is no response—only confused looks. Finally, Larry raises his hand.]

TEACHER: Yes, Larry?

LARRY: Do you mean, get a drink right now?

TEACHER: Sure, right now. Would you like a drink?

LARRY: Why not?

TEACHER: Fine, then go get your drink of water.

[Larry gets up from his desk and heads for the door. Other students chuckle. Larry begins to open the door.]

TEACHER: Larry! What are you doing?

LARRY: I'm going to get a drink of water. You said I could.

TEACHER: I know that, but what are you doing right now?

LARRY: I'm opening the door.

TEACHER: Did I say you could open the door?

LARRY: No, but. . . .

TEACHER: But what?

LARRY: Well, how am I going to get a drink without opening the door?

TEACHER: So, you think it's okay to open the door if it's okay to get a drink. Is that right?

LARRY: Sure, I guess so.

TEACHER: Even though I didn't specifically say you could?

LARRY: Yes, but you did say I could get a drink!

TEACHER: Go on, then—get your drink.

[Larry leaves the room and returns after about 20 seconds. Heads for his desk.]

TEACHER: Larry! Where did you do?

LARRY: I got a drink of water!

TEACHER: Where?

LARRY: Just right outside.

TEACHER: Why didn't you go to the other end of the building to get your drink?

LARRY: Because you would have gotten mad at me.

TEACHER: Did I say you could get a drink?

LARRY: Yes.

TEACHER: Did I say you had to go to the nearest water fountain?

LARRY: No.

TEACHER: Sit down, Larry. *[Shifts focus to address the rest of the class.]* I told Larry that he could get a drink of water, and he proceeded to open the door, even though I didn't tell him he could. But he didn't go to a far-away fountain even though I did not say that he couldn't. Why did Larry think it was okay to open the door, but not okay to go to the other end of the building to get a drink? What's the difference?

SUE: He assumed that it was okay to open the door, but not okay to go down the hall.

TEACHER: "Assumed"—What do you mean?

SUE: Well, you know, it only makes sense to open the door to get a drink, but it doesn't make sense to go to the other end.

TEACHER: Why not?

SUE: He *has* to open the door to get a drink, but he doesn't *have* to go to the other end.

TEACHER: I see. It was necessary to open the door, but not necessary to go to the other end.

SUE: Yes, that's right.

TEACHER: What if the nearest water fountain isn't working? In fact, what if the *only* fountain that *is* working is at the other end of the building? Therefore, in order to get a drink, it would be *necessary* to go to the other end. Right?

PHIL: Yes.

TEACHER: Under those circumstances, would it have been okay for Larry to go to the other end to get a drink, which might take 10 to 15 minutes, without asking first?

[The class begins to debate the issue among themselves.]

TEACHER: Mary?

MARY: I don't think so. You wouldn't like that.

TEACHER: So, even though it would be *necessary,* Larry shouldn't just assume he can do it.

BILL: I disagree. You told him he could get a drink. He had to open the door.

TEACHER: It was necessary.

BILL: Yes, and it was also necessary to go to the other end. That's why it would be okay to do.

TEACHER: What do you think about that, Mary?

MARY: Well, you have to be reasonable. I still don't think you meant that he could go anywhere to get a drink of water.

TEACHER: Bill, let's take an extreme situation. Suppose no fountains worked. The water in the building was shut off. Would it have been okay for Larry to leave the building to get a drink?

BILL: No, of course not.

TEACHER: Unreasonable?

BILL: Yes.

TEACHER: So, what are we saying? If I tell Larry he can get a drink of water, then what can he assume that he can do?

BILL: Whatever is necessary, as long as it is reasonable.

TEACHER: Do you agree, Mary?

MARY: Yes, but I guess I disagree with Bill as to what is "reasonable."

TEACHER: I think that's right. *[Turns from Mary to the class as a whole.]* Now, what does this have to do with government? Yesterday, we talked about the functions of a constitution. One of those functions was to delegate powers to the government. Can anyone recall some of the powers that the U.S. Constitution specifically gives to the national government?

[Several students mention a few of the enumerated powers.]

TEACHER: That's good. Turn to Section 8 of Article I. Here you will find a listing of these powers which are called "expressed" or "enumerated" powers because they are specifically mentioned in the Constitution.

[The teacher reads through the list, reviewing the meaning of the key terms.]

TEACHER: Now, I would like for you to think again about Larry and his problem in getting a drink of water. Suppose that I'm the Constitution. What is Larry?

PHIL: Larry is the government.

TEACHER: Which government?

PHIL: The national government.

TEACHER: Why?

PHIL: Because the Constitution gives power to the national government, like you said. And you gave power to Larry when you said he could get a drink of water.

TEACHER: So, Larry's power to get a drink is an example of what kind of power?

JIM: It's an enumerated power because that's what you specifically said he could do.

TEACHER: Then, if that's true, what kind of power was it to "open the door"?

JIM: It's an "assumed power." Larry assumed he could open the door.

TEACHER: Even though I, the Constitution, didn't specifically say that Larry, the government, could. Is that right?

MARY: Yes, because we agreed that it was a necessary and reasonable thing to do.

TEACHER: So, I implied that he could do more than I specifically said he could do.

BILL: Yes.

TEACHER: Does the Constitution imply that the national government can do more than is enumerated? Is there anything in the Constitution to suggest that the government may assume certain powers not specifically granted to it?

[No response.]

TEACHER: Okay, look at the last paragraph of Section 8. Jim read it please.

JIM: "To make all laws which shall be necessary and proper for carrying into execution the foregoing powers. . . ."

TEACHER: That's enough. Thanks, Jim. Now, what do you think is the purpose of this section?

RECONSTRUCTING EVENTS BEHIND *MARBURY v. MADISON*

Karen Tryda

Introduction

This activity undertakes to bring the important case of *Marbury v. Madison* to life for students through an imaginary historical drama. John Adams, John Marshall, and James Madison are the principal characters in this brief play, which is intended for students to read aloud or act out in class. The dramatization can provide a point of entry to detailed study of *Marbury v. Madison,* acquainting students with its basic facts. It is designed to prepare and motivate students to research the case and explore the consequences of the precedent it set. The activity includes a "*Marbury v. Madison* Puzzle" that serves as a recall exercise for students after reading or performing the play.

Depending upon students' abilities, teachers might conclude the activity by asking students to analyze the characterizations and situations in this little drama. Do these portraits and events seem accurate or likely to the students, insofar as they have any knowledge upon which to base an opinion? Teachers can discuss with students how useful they think it is to recreate and dramatize events in history in this way.

Procedure

As preparation for formal study of *Marbury v. Madison:*

1. Distribute a copy of the play to each student.
2. Assign parts, and have students read or dramatize the fictionalized account of events.
3. Discuss the following key questions:
   - Why were the Republicans anxious to prevent the appointment of the Federalist judges?
   - What precedent did the ruling in *Marbury v. Madison* establish?
   - What effect did Marshall's decision have upon the power of the courts?
   - Why is the power of judicial review still important to us today?
   - How is judicial review used today?
4. Ask students to read the account of *Marbury v. Madison* provided in their textbook, or provide other information about the case.
5. Discuss the long-term impact of Marshall's decision.
6. Distribute the "*Marbury v. Madison* Puzzle," and ask students to solve it.

THE CASE OF THE "MIDNIGHT JUDGES"

CHARACTERS:

JOHN ADAMS, outgoing President of the United States

JOHN MARSHALL, Secretary of State to John Adams and newly appointed Chief Justice of the Supreme Court

JAMES MADISON, Secretary of State to Thomas Jefferson
JAMES GERALD, secretary to John Marshall
RICHARD, butler to Thomas Jefferson
EDNA, maid to Thomas Jefferson
1st MAN, messenger
2nd MAN, messenger

SCENE ONE

[The office of the President, John Adams. The year is 1800.]

MR. GERALD *[running into the room with a stack of papers]:* Mr. Adams, Mr. Adams, we have finished all the letters of commission for the new judges. You need only to sign them.

JOHN ADAMS *[sitting at his large desk smiling, takes the letters, and begins signing them]:* Very good, James. Please take them to Mr. Marshall for distribution.

GERALD *[nervously]:* Yes, sir. I will hurry, but I don't know how we will get them all delivered before you have to leave office. That Mr. Jefferson will be very angry when he sees *all* these appointments. Yes, indeed!

ADAMS *[calmly]:* If you don't hurry, James, he'll have nothing to be angry about.

[James Gerald hurries out of the room and goes to the office of John Marshall, Secretary of State to John Adams.]

SCENE TWO

[The office of John Marshall.]

GERALD *[excitedly]:* Mr. Marshall, I have finished the letters and secured the President's signature.

JOHN MARSHALL *[looks up from his work and scowls at Mr. Gerald]:* James, you must not be so excitable. This is all in a day's work. Now, place the seal on each, and begin delivery. Time is running out. President Adams wishes that all of these new positions for judges be filled with Federalists—as we are doing. If we delay, there will be trouble.

[Quietly, James Gerald affixes the seals on each commission, places the documents in a pouch, and disappears from the room.]

MARSHALL *[left alone, thinking aloud]:* I wonder if this can be done as the President wishes? I wonder if I will be a good Chief Justice of the Supreme Court? There is so much to do. I cannot believe that I am sitting here holding two positions! Mr. Adams is an interesting man.

SCENE THREE

[Thomas Jefferson has assumed the Presidency. James Madison has been appointed as his Secretary of State. The scene opens at the President's house.]

RICHARD: That Mr. Jefferson sure is a nice man. He shakes hands with everybody and treats everyone the same way—just like they were "folks."

EDNA: He does seem nice. It's too bad his wife isn't alive to enjoy the President's parties, but that Mrs. Madison—Dolley, he calls her—makes a wonderful hostess. She treats Mr. Jefferson like he was her father. *[moving off to another room]* Yes, sir—nice people!

[There is a knock at the door. Richard opens it to let in two gentlemen.]

1st MAN *[without removing his hat, begins to speak in an excited voice]:* It is urgent that we speak to Mr. Jefferson or Mr. Madison at once!

2nd MAN: Yes, we *must* see one of them right away! We've come on very serious business.

RICHARD *[displeased with the commotion]:* May I take your hats, sirs?

1st and 2nd MEN *[protesting impatiently]:* Don't bother with our hats; just tell them we are here.

RICHARD: Very well, sirs. The President is not in right now, but Mr. Madison is in the other room. I'll tell him you are here.

[Richard leaves the room and returns quickly with James Madison following closely behind him.]

JAMES MADISON *[surprised]:* Gentlemen, how are you?

1st MAN: Not at all well at the moment. We are just ahead of William Marbury's lawyers. They are about to seek a Writ of Mandamus that will force you to deliver those commissions for Adams' "midnight judges."

MADISON *[growing angry as he speaks]:* Don't worry, gentlemen. Even if they do try to force me to do that, I won't. That was an underhanded trick that Mr. Adams tried to play—putting all those Federalist judges into office when he lost the election. They can't make me do it!!

2nd MAN: All right, Mr. Madison, you do as you please, but we did want to warn you—there will be trouble, you know. Good day, sir.

[Both men turn and leave.]

MADISON *[pacing up and down, muttering to himself]:* I know that these commissions are very important to William Marbury and his Federalist friends, but I cannot allow John Adams to succeed in this. If these Federalists become judges, they will have complete control of the courts. It must not happen!!

SCENE FOUR

[Several weeks later. There is a pounding at the door of Thomas Jefferson's house, and Richard answers it. Seeing the two gentlemen standing there again causes him to frown.]

RICHARD: Yes, may I help you?

1st MAN *[pushing his way past Richard, with the second man at his heels]:* Get Mr. Madison immediately!

RICHARD: May I take your hats, sirs?

[Both men glare at Richard. With dignity, he turns and goes to Madison's office.]

MADISON *[rushing into the room]:* News, my good men? What news have you heard?

2nd MAN: Mr. Madison, something remarkable has happened.

[The three of them move closer together in intense conversation.]

1st MAN: You know, sir, that William Marbury asked the Supreme Court to issue a Writ of Mandamus against you. The writ would force you to hand over the commissions. He believed that the Judiciary Act of 1789 gave him that right.

2nd MAN: Yes, and we thought that he would certainly get it. After all, John Marshall is the Chief Justice, and *he* was appointed by John Adams.

1st MAN *[angrily]:* That Judiciary Act has been the source of all the trouble anyway. It was the Judiciary Act that gave Adams the power to choose judges for these new positions. And with them, the Federalists would certainly have property claims and disputes decided their way.

MADISON *[impatiently]:* Never mind all that now, gentlemen. Please, tell me what has happened.

1st MAN: Well, Chief Justice Marshall decided that Mr. Marbury and his friends Ramsay, Harper, and Hooe did have a right to the Writ of Mandamus. . .

MADISON *[interrupting]:* Oh, no!! How could he. . .

1st MAN *[interrupting Madison]:* Wait, Mr. Madison—I'm not finished. John Marshall said they did have a right to the writ as far as the law was concerned, but that he wouldn't issue it!!

MADISON *[dumbfounded]:* Why not? Why ever not?

2nd MAN: Chief Justice Marshall said that the Judiciary Act, which allowed for the writs, was not in agreement with the Constitution. . .

1st MAN *[interrupting again]:* And, any law that is in conflict with the Constitution must be thrown out. We've won! We've won!!

[James Madison is speechless for a time, while he considers the implications of John Marshall's decision.]

MADISON: This is wonderful. This means an end to it. *[hesitates, then looks questioningly into the eyes of his visitors]* Or is it?? This could be only a beginning. This is the first time a law has ever been declared unconstitutional. I wonder where this novel idea will take us? *[Shaking his head from side to side, he ushers the two men, now quiet, to the door.]* Yes, I wonder. Judicial review of laws made by Congress. . . . What an extraordinary idea!

MARBURY v. MADISON PUZZLE

1. J___ ________
2. _U_____ _____
3. _____ __D____
4. _I______ ______
5. __C______
6. ____I____
7. _______ _A_____
8. ____L___
9. R_________
10. _E_________
11. _______V_ ______
12. ______I___ ___
13. ______ _E_______
14. W___ __ ________

1. The justice who issued the ruling in the *Marbury v. Madison* case.
2. The court which holds the power to declare laws unconstitutional.
3. Thomas Jefferson's Secretary of State, who refused to deliver the commissions made by Adams.
4. Nickname for the judges appointed by Adams as he left office.
5. What we call the opinions set down by the Court.
6. If someone is granted a position in the government without winning an election, we say that he is ___?___.
7. The plaintiff in the *Marbury v. Madison* case.
8. When two views cannot be brought into agreement, we say that they are in ___?___.
9. The political party represented by Jefferson.
10. The political party represented by John Adams.
11. The branch of government that would be the receiver of the writs issued under the Judiciary Act of 1789.
12. A law passed in 1789 which allowed for the issuance of a Writ of Mandamus.
13. The president of the U.S. when this case was decided.
14. An order from the court that would have forced Madison to deliver the commissions.

KEY TO PUZZLE

1. **J**OHN MARSHALL
2. S**U**PREME COURT
3. JAMES MA**D**ISON
4. M**I**DNIGHT JUDGES
5. DE**C**ISIONS
6. APPO**I**NTED
7. WILLIAM M**A**RBURY
8. CONF**L**ICT

9. **R**EPUBLICANS
10. F**E**DERALISTS
11. EXECUTI**V**E BRANCH
12. JUDICI**I**ARY ACT
13. THOMAS J**E**FFERSON
14. **W**RIT OF MANDAMUS

RE-TRYING *McCULLOCH v. MARYLAND*

Rosemary V. Miller and Susan M. Darnley

Introduction

In the early years of the republic, the Supreme Court frequently found itself in the middle of an ongoing struggle for power between the states and the national government. This power struggle often manifested itself in conflict between Americans who favored a broad interpretation of the Constitution and those who favored a strict construction. A broad interpretation, or "loose construction," of the Constitution of course gives many "implied powers" to the national government, while a "strict construction" reserves many powers to the states. The case of *McCulloch v. Maryland* illustrates the unsettled nature of early federalism in the United States.

The Second Bank of the United States had been created by Congress without controversy in 1816. Its purpose was to serve as a depository for federal funds and to print bank notes. The federal government owned one-fifth of the Bank's stock, and private investors held the rest. The Bank was given the power to establish branches in principal cities and towns.

The Bank engaged in some speculative activities and fraudulent banking practices. Correcting these adversely affected several southern and western states, which retaliated by prohibiting the Bank from operating within their borders, or by taxing it heavily.

The state of Maryland attempted to drive the bank from its domain by imposing a stiff tax, which the Baltimore branch of the Bank chose to ignore. Maryland then sued the Bank's cashier, James McCulloch, and won its case in the state's courts. McCulloch appealed the Bank's case to the Supreme Court.

This activity divides the class into three groups of students to re-argue and re-decide the case of *McCulloch v. Maryland.* The activity should be carried out *prior to* studying Chief Justice John Marshall's actual decision in the case. One group of students will argue the case for the plaintiff, McCulloch, while a second group will marshal the defense for the state of Maryland. A third group of students, acting as Supreme Court justices, will render an opinion deciding the case.

Procedure

1. Either by lecture or reading assignment, impart the historical context and facts of the case. *Do not disclose the decision in the case.*
2. In class discussion, elicit the constitutional issues raised by the case:
   - Which has sovereignty—the states acting separately (such as Maryland), or the people acting collectively (through Congress, in the establishment of the Bank)?
   - Does the Constitution give Congress the power to incorporate a bank?

- If so, does the Constitution reserve to a state the right to tax it?

3. Divide the class into three groups representing the federal government, the state of Maryland, and the Supreme Court.
4. Direct students to the relevant sections of the Constitution (Article I, Section 8, clauses 1–18; Article I, Section 10; Article VI, clause 2; and Amendment 10).
5. Provide each group with the Suggested Guide Questions. Remind students to use the facts of the case, logical reasoning, and the Constitution to support their arguments.
6. Allow each side to present its case to the justices. Students assigned to build a case for the Bank can argue that Congress's authority to establish the Bank is implied by several of the powers delegated to it by the Constitution—the power to lay and collect taxes, to coin money and regulate its value, to borrow money, and to regulate commerce among the several states.

   Students assigned to defend the action of the state of Maryland can argue that there is no mention of a bank in the delegated powers and that the notion of "implied power" is nonsense. (This is what Attorney General Luther Martin of Maryland in fact did argue.) They can maintain that the only way for Maryland to stop this unconstitutional operation is to tax the bank out of existence.
7. Allow the justices to confer, make their decision(s), and present it (them) to the class. Students assigned to decide the case must address the three constitutional issues at stake.
8. To conclude the activity, have students read the actual decision and consider its arguments. John Marshall, an ardent supporter of the national judiciary and national supremacy, wrote the opinion for the majority. He upheld the constitutionality of Congress's authority to establish a bank, reasoning that the law creating the bank was "necessary and proper for carrying into execution" several expressed powers. "Let the end be legitimate, let it be within the scope of the constitution," and Congress may use "all means which are appropriate . . . which are not prohibited."

   Furthermore, Marshall ruled that Maryland could not tax the Second Bank of the United States without violating the Constitution. The Bank was within the national government's sphere of action and "the government of the Union, though limited in its powers, is supreme within its sphere of action." The Chief Justice added that "the power to tax involves the power to destroy." Therefore, the "states have no power, by taxation or otherwise, to retard, impede, burden, or in any manner control the operations of the constitutional laws enacted by Congress to carry into execution the powers vested in the general government."
9. Ask students to offer present-day examples of implied powers. (Students might mention regulation of television and radio stations, the Federal Reserve System, and grant-in-aid programs.)

SUGGESTED GUIDE QUESTIONS

1. What were the reasons for the creation of the Bank, and what problems were associated with it?

2. Is the power to create a bank specifically mentioned or implied in the Constitution?
3. Is the use of "implied power" by the national government dangerous?
4. Are there any restrictions on the power of a state to tax such a bank? Are there problems with a state taking such action?

APPLYING AND ENFORCING THE THIRTEENTH AMENDMENT

Stephanie Zaidman

Introduction

The Thirteenth Amendment was passed by Congress in January of 1865. The states ratified it in December of the same year, with the assistance of eight southern states. This amendment outlawed slavery and involuntary servitude, except as punishment for convicted criminals. In a second section of the amendment, Congress proclaimed for itself the power to pass laws that would overrule or ignore laws passed by the states, if necessary, to enforce the amendment.

Passage of this amendment came naturally and logically upon the close of the Civil War. In the course of subsequent events, however, the Thirteenth Amendment was largely superseded by the Fourteenth, which was ratified in 1868 and has been widely used to secure protection of minority rights from both the federal and state governments. Nevertheless, it was the Thirteenth Amendment that represented a dramatic break with the past and the beginning of modern Constitutional interpretation, since it gives the federal government control over an area previously controlled by the states.

In this activity, students will be asked to consider two case studies and decide if the Thirteenth Amendment has any applicability to them. The first concerns the plight of an Alabama tenant farmer, and the second, the internment of Japanese-Americans during World War II. In examining both cases, students should give particular attention to the second section of the Thirteenth Amendment.

Procedure

1. In the process of teaching about the Constitution or the Civil War, guide students in studying the Thirteenth Amendment. Give special emphasis to Section 2, which gives Congress the power of enforcement.
2. Distribute the two case studies—"The Tenant Farmer" and "Japanese-Americans Interned." Students can work on the case studies by themselves, they can read them aloud and discuss them as a class, or they can consider one or both of them in small groups.
3. Ask students to answer the following questions:
   - What might be done to solve the problem presented by each case study?
   - How might the people involved in each situation appeal for protection under the Thirteenth Amendment?
   - How does each of these situations compare and/or contrast with slavery?

CASE STUDY 1: THE TENANT FARMER

Isaiah Potts, his wife, and their four children lived in rural Alabama. They farmed 50 acres of land owned by George Grimes, who had six other families farming other portions of his land, as well.

When Isaiah began farming, he had no money or farm equipment. Mr. Grimes agreed to provide the seed and equipment necessary to plant the first cotton crop, in return for a portion of the crop. Another portion was to be given as rent for the land and the shack in which the family would live. Unable to write his name, Isaiah made his mark on the contract drawn up by Mr. Grimes.

The work was endless backbreaking labor. Isaiah and his two oldest boys were up at dawn and often didn't finish until sundown. In the first year, there was too much rain, which ruined a portion of the crop. Then one of the boys was injured, which made the picking progress very slowly. In the end, the crop was not large enough to pay off Grimes and support the Potts family as well. Extra work was hard to find, and eventually Isaiah was forced to go to Mr. Grimes and borrow against the next year's crop—a common practice among tenant farmers.

Over the next several years, this pattern continued. Isaiah's harvests were insufficient to pay his debts, and he was forced to borrow more and more money from George Grimes. Eventually, Isaiah decided that the only thing to do was to leave the land and move to the North, where there were factory jobs available.

Isaiah went to Mr. Grimes to tell him of the decision to move. Mr. Grimes pulled out his ledger book and looked to see what Isaiah owed. When Grimes showed the amount to Isaiah, he was overwhelmed! He could never pay back that much—not if he worked for fifty more years. Neither he nor his children would ever be able to repay Grimes, and thus they would be tied to the land forever.

CASE 2: JAPANESE-AMERICANS INTERNED

In 1942, an executive order issued by Franklin Roosevelt required that the Japanese-Americans living in California along the Pacific Coast be isolated and interned at camps located inland. They had little time to sell their homes and arrange their business affairs, and they were allowed to take very few possessions with them to the camps. The rest of their goods and property were forfeited to the government. They were loaded into trucks and taken away to their wartime quarters.

Most of the camps consisted of huge barracks surrounded by barbed wire and patrolled by National Guardsmen. Though family members remained together, the accommodations were rough and uncomfortable.

Those in the camps were expected to earn their keep by working in a variety of jobs, including cleaning the barracks and farming. Some were set to work at very menial tasks in the kitchens and storerooms. Some of the younger men were eventually released from the camps to join the armed forces, even while their loyalty was questioned. The vast majority, however, remained in the internment camps until 1945.

Part III

The Twentieth Century

CHAPTER 4

DEVELOPING THE CONSTITUTION AS WE KNOW IT

Howard N. Meyer and Michael Solliday

The evolution of the Constitution during the twentieth century follows two connected branches. The first branch tracks the transformation of the office of the president and the accompanying growth of federal power and responsibility in economic and personal concerns. The second branch pursues the gradually regenerated Fourteenth Amendment, making what, in sports parlance, would be called its "comeback." The Fourteenth Amendment now touches on many aspects of our lives and is the focus of as much as half of all constitutional litigation. Protection against power's abuse is its central function.

The recurrent theme along both branches is sounded by the Bill of Rights. The "rights" in question are the privileges and immunities embodied in the first ten amendments. Moreover, gaining importance and recognition for the first time in this century is the unambiguous declaration in the Ninth Amendment that rights may be found to exist and be granted protection that are nowhere specifically mentioned in the Constitution.

There have been some significant changes in the Constitution that were promulgated by the formal amending process. But these are relatively less important than changes in its meaning brought about by court decision or presidential practice. A judicial Rip Van Winkle who had slept for eighty-seven years would rub his or her eyes in disbelief, utterly at a loss to understand the major alterations in the Constitution's content that have come about without any change in its text.

The essence of what we had in 1900, with respect to the "people-connected" aspects of the Constitution, was described rather well during the Bicentennial of the Declaration of 1776. By "people-connected" aspects, we mean those private, human benefits promised in the Preamble: "establish Justice," "promote the general Welfare," and "secure the Blessings of Liberty." At a special 1976 meeting of the American Academy of Political and Social Science, the keynote speaker, Louis Pollak, then Dean of the University of Pennsylvania Law School and now a federal judge, declared:

> The America which came of age in 1900 was an anomalous polity. The Constitution . . . was at last obsolete. It was a Constitution sedulously protective of the racist

instincts of the many and the acquisitive instincts of the few. It was a Constitution with little feeling for the "truths" proclaimed in 1776.

In contrast, what we have now—with a few painful exceptions—is an aggregate of limitations on the power of the government to do harm and a charter of authority of government to serve the general welfare of the people which may be equalled, but is not excelled anywhere. Very few of us, given a choice, would prefer to live under the United States Constitution as it was construed in 1900.

The century began with the Court primed to continue the activism that it had shown in overturning state laws that justices construed as impairing "liberty" by their effect on business practices or prices. Overturning *federal* action by narrow interpretation of commerce power was another sort of judicial activism that protected "the acquisitive instincts of the few," to use Dean Pollak's phrase. Such activism was notoriously absent when it came to cases where the actual purposes of the Fourteenth should have been furthered. The pattern for the immediate future was set by the Court's refusal to interfere with state-compelled segregation in the *Plessy* case.

Plessy v. Ferguson was the "law of the land" for over half of the twentieth century. Decided in 1896, this case became the most famous betrayal of the Fourteenth Amendment, but it did not stand alone. It was the culminating indignity of a series of nineteenth-century decisions through which the Court frustrated the purposes of the Amendment. The framers of the Fourteenth Amendment had found that the abolition of slavery was by itself insufficient to end its evils. Investigation by the Congressional Joint Committee on Reconstruction had confirmed evidence of widespread violation of a variety of rights by the states. When the Committee members hammered out the Fourteenth Amendment, they believed that it would graft onto the Constitution federal guarantees of both equality and justice, of civil rights *and* civil liberties.

The expectation of the framers of the Fourteenth Amendment that it would provide national protection against state wrongs was disappointed in case after case. The process of judicial nullification began in 1873 with the *Slaughterhouse* decision, which established the pattern of ignoring the congressional decision to distrust state discretion in human rights matters. *Plessy,* which symbolized for so long the Court's—and the nation's—indifference to the rights of blacks was the logical sequel to that first ruling.

The Court's sophistry, reinforced by a complex of socioeconomic factors, confounded legal scholarship and conventional wisdom for some time. Nonetheless, change was persistently pushed from below. One has only to read the words of the Fourteenth Amendment in the context of history to perceive the framers' intent. Twentieth-century history has been marked by a chipping away and ultimate overthrow of the abuse of judicial power. But this process did not begin for another decade and a half.

What *Plessy* promised about the temper of the Court was delivered in further cases in the opening decade of the twentieth century. In a 1903 opinion written by Justice Holmes, the Court let stand one of the segregation states' many schemes, piled up to bar black voting. The plain violation of the Voting Rights

Amendment—the Fifteenth—as well as the equal protection pledge guaranteed by the Fourteenth Amendment were disregarded. A few years later, a nasty barrier was imposed on purely voluntary interracial association. Kentucky's Berea College had flourished as an oasis of brotherhood, accepting registrants regardless of color, until it was restrained by the brute force of a state law. In 1907, the Supreme Court allowed this, with Holmes silently concurring and John Marshall Harlan of Kentucky, the great nineteenth-century dissenter, objecting with his usual vigor.

In its failure to act when activism was its constitutional duty, the Court was not alone, nor of course was it "bucking" majority opinion in a society receptive to racism. It was incumbent upon Congress, under the second clause of the Fourteenth Amendment, in its post-census reallocation of House seats, to reduce representation in proportion to the percentage of voting-right denials. The only serious attempt to fulfill this obligation occurred in 1901. Legal and extra-legal devices for disfranchisement had gradually reduced black representation in the House to one last member. A fight for a motion to instruct the Committee on the Census to perform the congressional duty to reduce seats in offending states failed. The shame of the House of Representatives was enhanced when it was reminded of the record of valor of the black regiments of the then so recent Spanish-American War.

That war, duly declared against Spain, was followed by the first large-scale combat without a congressional declaration (except for the various campaigns against native American tribes). Events in the Philippines provided the occasion. The Philippine islands were a Spanish colony whose native population had by guerrilla warfare nearly won their goal of nationhood and self-determination on their own. Though the native rebels against Spanish rule had helped our naval forces take and hold Manila, they were in sole control of the rest of the islands. After a Spanish surrender and armistice, President McKinley, upon the urging of his assistant Navy Secretary, Theodore Roosevelt, ordered our troops—no longer authorized to continue the declared war against Spain—to fight the guerilla forces of the incipient nation.

Opposition on moral grounds to this "war of conquest," as the consensus of our historians judge it, was voiced by a substantial segment of the population, including populists, intellectuals, and old abolitionists, who perceived the racist component of the administration's decision to deny self-determination to the Philippines. The Anti-Imperialist League led the dissent, which was not made a judicial question by litigation, and was defeated politically in the 1900 election. The freedom fighters were crushed by American troops, and the islands were annexed, as were Puerto Rico and some others.

No precedent was thus furnished that would be relevant to the current ongoing debate about our frequent launching of hostilities without authorization by Congress through its exclusive power to *declare* war. The annexations of new colonies did revive issues that our westward expansion and acquisition of intra-continental territory had presented. Previously acquired territory, however, was understood, by common consent, to be eligible for statehood on terms of parity with previously existing or organized states of the union.

The question "Does the Constitution follow the flag?" was presented in several aspects as the United States behaved for the first time in its history as a colonial power, proceeding with a certain amnesia—analogous to the amnesia that the nation exhibited in its internal affairs—about the principles that were enunciated in the 1776 Declaration. In deciding a group of so-called Insular Cases after the crucial 1900 election, the Supreme Court held that the Constitution's opening words, "We, the People . . ." did not preclude the taking of territory where the inhabitants could not be deemed to be part of the first-class citizen population of the United States, and that the question of whether the new subjects had any rights under the Constitution would in each case be deferred until Congress acted to declare them "incorporated"—a word nowhere mentioned in the Constitution or any amendment. F. P. Dunne, then a popular columnist-commentator, had his persona Mr. Dooley declare that he was not sure whether the Constitution followed the flag, but that the Supreme Court apparently followed the "ilection" returns.

Theodore Roosevelt, who had acted as the co-founder of what could be called the first American Empire even before he became Vice-President, took office when McKinley was assassinated. His accession marked the first of two basic changes in the nature of the presidency. These changes were neither intended by the framers, nor resulted from changes in wording. Professor Alpheus T. Mason has suggested that three "striking and divergent" theories of the presidency have prevailed: the "constitutional," the "stewardship," and the "prerogative" theories. Except for the tragic times during which Abraham Lincoln presided, the constitutional theory had customarily prevailed. The presidential office-holder had limited himself to the powers spelled out in the document or necessarily implied from them.

With the aggressive, active, and extroverted first Roosevelt—the "steward of the people," as Theodore Roosevelt styled himself—something new was added. He thought he could do, in his words, "anything that the needs of the nation demanded unless such action was forbidden by the Constitution and the laws." His successor, William Howard Taft, repudiated such authority, but Woodrow Wilson reclaimed it when he succeeded Taft. After Wilson led the nation into the war of 1917–18, he went further and set the precedent as wartime leader that Franklin D. Roosevelt was to follow in the national emergency of the Great Depression of 1929–33. FDR's version of presidential authority, as viewed by Professor Mason, conformed to John Locke's concept of prerogative: "the power to act according to discretion for the public good, without the prescription of the law and sometimes even against it."

As the new century got under way, leadership of the forces of reform passed from the militantly discontented populist movements of the late nineteenth century to the less strident and seemingly more "respectable" Progressives. As one historian has suggested—a bit more colorfully than accurately—the new crop of advocates of change wore shirts, ties, and socks. The emergence of the so-called "muckraking" periodicals, in which some of the less attractive consequences of unbridled capitalism were quite vividly portrayed, helped to make the liberal programs of the era acceptable. They seemed less threatening now than the earlier movements that had led some Supreme Court justices to use the power of the Court to protect their former clients from socialism or worse.

In this new climate, enough support was mustered in 1913 to ratify two Constitutional amendments. The Sixteenth was the Income Tax Amendment, and the Seventeenth changed the Constitution's flawed provision for election of United States senators. This was the year's major contribution to American democracy. By this amendment, senators were to be elected by the people directly, instead of by the state legislatures, which were sometimes prone to corruption or control by the railroads or other strong business interests.

During this period, the Supreme Court acquiesced in amendments to the regulatory laws designed to restore features that the Court had nullified by earlier restrictive interpretations of the commerce clause. (As Professor Edward S. Corwin has pointed out, when the Court later came to consider the array of New Deal laws, the justices had two alternate sets of interpretations of the clause to choose between, and following either, they could say they were in accord with precedent.) Likewise, beginning with decisions in some tariff cases and then extending to other fields, the Court permitted a variety of the features of the independent-agency form of government regulation, which was then in its infancy. These included the delegation of legislative or executive authority, the power to make rules that would control specific spheres of activity, and criminal law enforcement sanctions. The states continued to be tightly restrained by a veto power that grew in the 1920s.

Under Theodore Roosevelt, the machinery of governmental regulation of economic activity took on new life. Pursuing his view of his "stewardship," he engaged in personal acts of intervention in domestic affairs without regard to constitutional specification of the scope of his powers or duties. He initiated the use of information-gathering commissions, and launched the first round of conservation efforts—what we think of now under the broader label of environmental protection. He sallied forth in foreign affairs in a fashion unprecedented in the nation's previous hemispherically provincial history—a fashion suitable for a newly born empire, and not forbidden—if not precisely authorized, either—by the Constitution. One fruit of Roosevelt's efforts was a Nobel Peace Prize for helping to end the Russo-Japanese War.

His successful rudimentary stabs at making the presidency the focal point of the operation of the national government were followed up by Woodrow Wilson, a former professor of political science who had entered partisan politics and succeeded. Long before the century began, he had written a treatise offering an unfriendly critique of what his title identified as *Congressional Government.* During his presidency, Wilson developed to its highest level executive intrusion into the legislative process. This intrusion consisted in formulating legislative programs and campaigning for their adoption, by lobbying and "going to the people" to put pressure on Congress. If this was not a violation of what the 1787 framers had provided, it was certainly not part of their original intention for the office. Well before Wilson led the nation into World War I and took charge of all significant economic activity on behalf of the federal government, he had put forward a program under the slogan of "New Freedom" that created a number of new regulatory agencies now constituting part of the bureaucratic state.

Two less familiar features of the Wilson administration were symptomatic of the nation's continuance in the path charted in *Plessy v. Ferguson,* chief symbol of federal refusal to accept and apply the principles of the Fourteenth Amendment. Born in Georgia in 1856, Wilson had gone to college and law school in the immediate aftermath of the end of the Reconstruction reforms and the restoration of white supremacy in the former slave states. He was imbued with counter-Reconstruction prejudices, and he rationalized racism by accepting distorted versions of the history of slavery and abolitionism, and the Civil War and Reconstruction. He saw no evil in introducing segregation into offices of the United States government and authorized that disgraceful action. And when film-maker D. W. Griffith made *Birth of a Nation,* his epic dramatization of the novel, *The Clansman,* glorifying the Ku Klux Klan—and incidentally contributing to its first revival—Wilson arranged for a White House premiere and praised the film as "history written with lightning."

When Homer Plessy had been arrested and charged with riding in a white man's car, his action had been one of deliberate defiance instigated by a branch of the resistance movement of his day. The movement defended him, and his case was taken to the Supreme Court by its attorneys. Following in the tradition of that movement, the Niagara Movement was formed by a group of black intellectuals early in the twentieth century under the leadership of W.E.B. DuBois. DuBois proclaimed that "We want the Constitution of the country enforced. . . . We want our children educated. . . . We want justice even for criminals and outlaws. . . . The battle we wage is not for ourselves alone, but for all true Americans." This last declaration was demonstrated when his group merged with many liberal and socialist whites to form the National Association for the Advancement of Colored People.

Recognizing that the problem was more than laws and customs alone, the NAACP launched an unsuccessful effort to combat the pernicious motion picture *Birth of a Nation,* which the President had endorsed. Although unsuccessful, the campaign was not entirely futile, as the continuing controversy over the film and the version of history that it represented had some effect on the public opinion in which constitutional law is generated.

In the immediate aftermath of its fight over the Griffith movie, the NAACP enjoyed its initial successes in the Supreme Court in the long fight to regenerate the Fourteenth Amendment and the voting rights pledge extended by the Fifteenth. These rulings declared the unconstitutionality of the restrictive covenant device for residential segregation and the "grandfather clause." Under the "grandfather clause," a black man was exempt from passing a rigged literacy test as a qualification for voting if his grandfather had voted. However, his grandfather most likely had been a slave. These rulings were largely ineffectual in their day, but they were the first steps in the "long march" that ultimately led to the school desegregation decisions and beyond.

The ending of municipally enacted residential segregation contained the germs of the inevitable *Brown* ruling forty years later. On every side the effort was pressed—jobs, votes, housing, and, above all, education. There were setbacks along the road. The full tale is told elsewhere. It is worth pausing to stress a point made by constitutional scholar Alfred H. Kelly. While no admirer of Earl Warren, Kelly nevertheless concedes that "the Warren Court has not been the creator of the major doctrines" for which it has been praised and blamed. The "seeds" of the *Brown* case "were sown in the very doctrine it overruled . . . when the American people were satisfied to pay only lip service to [*Plessy*] . . . to adhere to the privilege of separation but never to the duty of equality."

Charles L. Black, Jr., who was more sympathetic to the Warren Court than Kelly, gave the *Brown* decision a bit too much credit. "*Brown* knocked down the wall . . . ," he said, to describe the efficacy of Court rulings. But *Brown* was only part of the story. It did not sweep segregation away singlehandedly, but it flashed the signal. The wall came tumbling down after decades of militant activism by black people and their white allies—a struggle bathed in the blood of leaders like Martin Luther King, Jr., and Medgar Evers. And now there is a restored Constitution which a Rip Van Winkle waking from a sleep that began in 1900 couldn't possibly imagine.

The second chapter of the story of the redemption of the "equal" pledge of the Fourteenth Amendment involves the application of its sweeping assurance of equality of treatment beyond the racial minority for which it was originally intended. The framers of the Fourteenth Amendment—who knew the meaning of words and were very conscious of the great Declaration of 1776 as they wrote—did not in any way confine it to this minority, however. "All persons"—the words chosen in 1866 to signify what the framers thought was meant by "all men" in 1776—came gradually to include those denied equality of treatment because they were poor, or aliens, or those of so-called "illegitimate" birth, or, to a certain extent, those unorthodox in politics or sexuality, or old, or young, or physically handicapped.

In addition, "all persons" came to apply to women. During Woodrow Wilson's administration, the long effort of the first and sometimes forgotten drive of the feminist movement was successful. Women had now secured the vote, as a recognition of their full personhood and as a base for completing the balance of their campaign for full equality. Contrary to their hopes and expectations, winning the vote secured little tangible gain in other areas which were controlled by male-dominated legislatures and courts that seemed to change attitude very little with the advent of the new voters. A new wave of feminism began in the 1960s, heralded by such cries as that voiced in the despairing title of an essay by Rochelle Girson, then Literary Editor of the *Saturday Review*—"What Did the Nineteenth Amendment Amend?"

Finally, in 1971 came the first of the Supreme Court rulings that women, too, were *persons* within the Fourteenth Amendment—persons who could not be denied the equal protection of the laws. A subsequent cascade of rulings reflected the extent to which male justices' consciousnesses had been raised by feminism's new wave and its arguments—and by the action, some thought, of Congress in passing by whopping majorities a proposed Equal Rights Amendment and sending it along to the states for the final step in the ratification process outlined in the basic law.

The First World War—for "democracy," as it was billed—and the Second—for "Four Freedoms"—each played a role in the long march towards the ideal of equality—an ideal that had to be seen to be realized, at least partially, if the sacrifices made in each war were not to be thought in vain. The role of women on the homefront in 1917–19 was important in the final push of the suffrage movement. Wartime events, in another way, gave new impetus to the recognition and enforcement of state safeguards of the Bill of Rights, which act as a backstop or safety net for the Fourteenth Amendment. Also playing its part was the civil rights movement itself, drawing public attention to the fact that blacks suffered disproportionately—and not in the South alone—from lawless enforcement of the law.

That phrase, "lawless enforcement of the law," was the title of one of the reports of the Wickersham Commission appointed by President Herbert Hoover to investigate what was considered to be a crisis in criminal law enforcement in the 1920s. The Commission's three-and-a-half million words of reports was epitomized in the phrase by which the Supreme Court seemed to be increasingly motivated in the decades to come: "respect for law"—fundamental to observance of the law—"could hardly be expected" if law enforcement officers "fail to observe law themselves."

The Wickersham Commission, headed by former President Taft's Attorney General, George W. Wickersham, was in a sense a by-product of the Prohibition Amendment (the Eighteenth, which was subsequently repealed by the Twenty-first). This Amendment was a unique attempt to implant a primarily sectarian moral judgment in our basic law. Its passage was related to World War I in that it was eased by a wartime "emergency" prohibition law intended to conserve grain for military purposes and for aid to the allies. The Commission, more than any other single force, can be seen as inspiring awareness of the need for a national supervisory role to guard against state court tolerance of violations of the protections against self-incrimination and the like.

More directly related to the war was the emergence of modern First Amendment civil liberties law. Repression of speech and related liberties by federal action, state action, and private panic reaction gave rise to extensive litigation, for the first time testing the extremely general protection afforded by the First Amendment. The Court declined to take literally (as several of its members in recent decades have argued that it should) the opening words, "Congress shall make *no* law. . . ." No federal curtailing of freedom of speech that was war-related was held by the Court to go too far, but a test imposing a limit was developed—the determination of "clear and present danger." Over the years this test has played no particular role in Court decisions, but has furnished a layperson's basis for lobbying against repressive proposals.

Reflecting the considerable war hysteria of the period 1917–20, states had launched prosecutions of their own and imposed other indignities that, viewed in the retrospect of the calmer days of the return to what President Harding called "normalcy," were seen to be shameful. The Supreme Court ultimately yielded to persistent argument in case after case that fundamental liberties should be protected against infringement by the states. These arguments echoed the need that prompted the Fourteenth Amendment: the need to protect abolitionist advocates and leaders of the freedmen. The Court finally ruled definitively that federal courts could ensure that states did not violate the First Amendment, by virtue of the Fourteenth's limitation on state action.

With the historic *Scottsboro* cases of the 1930s began the case-by-case recognition that the rest of the Bill of Rights needed guarding, via the Fourteenth Amendment, against lawlessness in state law enforcement. Though *Scottsboro* involved only the right to counsel as an essential ingredient of a fair trial and enforcement of equality by condemnation of all-white juries, these cases opened the door to a gradual setting of rules that effectuated what Wickersham had called for in 1930, most notably in his condemnation of the "third degree"—forced self-incrimination. The full fruit was harvested during Chief Justice Earl Warren's tenure, but the seeds had been planted thirty years previously in soil plowed and prepared in 1868 when the Fourteenth Amendment was ratified.

One far-reaching result of the revival of the Fourteenth Amendment's capacity to deliver equal protection should be given a separate starring position. The twentieth century has been marked by great shifts of population. In 1885, only one-third of Americans lived in cities; by 1960, two-thirds did. During most of these decades, many states failed to provide for fair apportionment of their voting districts. A county from which half the people had moved away might still have two legislators; another that had tripled in size with growth of its main city might continue to have only one. One vote in one county then might be worth six in the other. This pervasive inequality was confronted and eliminated in a series of rulings in the 1960s. The failure of local legislatures to remedy their own deficiencies (or that of their states' congressional representation) was dealt with as a denial of equal protection.

In many ways, then, the regeneration of the Fourteenth Amendment has helped to establish justice, secure the blessings of liberty, and even, in its effect on democracy, helped to bring about laws that advance the general welfare.

Shortly after the *Scottsboro* cases were decided, in the aftermath of the economic crisis that had caused the young defendants to climb on a freight train to travel to look for work, the Court excised from the Fourteenth Amendment what might be described as a growth—a growth that had never belonged there, but with which it had been identified almost exclusively as the century began. As part of what has justly been called the "constitutional revolution" of the late 1930s to early 1940s, the Court repudiated, as wrongfully seized, the power it had wielded under the Fourteenth Amendment's "due process of law" clause, which had been the pretext for nullifying laws providing for minimum wages, maximum hours, and a variety of other such reforms.

What has been referred to as the constitutional revolution of the late 1930s was a result of political conflict that followed a confrontation between the Supreme Court and President Franklin D. Roosevelt. The economic crisis that had begun in 1929 was more devastating than can now be imagined by those who did not live through it; in that pre-nuclear age, it was not thought extreme to compare it to a war emergency. Public opinion, not unreasonably, considered that responsibility lay largely with governmental laissez-faire attitudes toward business and with the tighter Court control and veto power over socioeconomic law-making that had prevailed in the 1920s. President Roosevelt's election was deemed a mandate for action, and spectacular action followed—a variety of laws and executive orders that collectively were known as the "New Deal."

When the Court struck down most of Roosevelt's economic reform program, the President retaliated with a program for Court reform. That failed in its tactical goal of opening the Court to new appointees by enlarging its membership; it succeeded in securing its strategic objective when the existing balance of power in the Court shifted. Final victory was assured as the "Old Guard" members of the Court retired, one by one. Soon the aberrations in constitutional interpretation that had prevailed since 1900, with respect to both state and federal power, had a decent burial.

Now federal power—including executive power—had a free rein. State authority, though shrunk by federal "pre-emption" (the notion that federal entry into commerce-connected and similar fields suspended state authority), was not likely to be challenged in the economic field by judicial ideas about unreasonableness.

The development of the law of constitutional liberty sagged in the 1950s, as more infringements of basic American freedoms were tolerated by the Court during the McCarthy phase of the Cold War than during the Second World War of 1941–1945. (One glaring exception marred World War II's record. That was the racist response to the attack on Pearl Harbor and the wrongful perception of a domestic threat after it succeeded. All American citizens of Japanese ancestry were ordered out of the West Coast states and detained indiscriminately for most of the rest of the war years. It was not an accepted rule of law at the time that the obligation to furnish equal protection of the law rested as much with the national government as it did with the states. The Fourteenth Amendment, indeed, spoke only of "states." Later, since one of the school desegregation cases came from the District of Columbia, governed by Congress at the time, the necessities of the cases obliged the Court to treat "equal protection" required by the Fifth Amendment's due process clause as a standard to which the federal government must adhere in all its activities.)

The Court's somewhat shaky record in civil liberties cases of the 1950s improved considerably when it was faced with the test of the Vietnam conflict and the widespread protests it evoked. Various manifestations of activist protest, ranging from the wearing of a mourning armband to school to a sweatshirt with an obscenity imprinted, presented some novel First Amendment issues, but were found to be within the dissenters' rights. Nevertheless, the Court backed off from taking a stand on the legality of the undeclared war, although at least four cases came up for review.

The shipment of substantial numbers of troops and much equipment to Korea could have been held to be legally defensible, as fulfillment of the treaty commitment that the United Nations Charter constituted. There is, after all, a clause in the Constitution that declares treaties to be part of the "supreme law of the land" (Article VI). In the case of Vietnam, Congress's anticipatory passage of the Gulf of Tonkin Resolution, plus congressional votes for appropriations, could have been deemed to be sufficient *de facto* substitutes for the constitutionally required declaration. (Former Law Dean and U.S. Senator Wayne Morse of Oregon opposed the Tonkin Gulf authorization as an unconstitutional blank check.) The Court's last refusal came after the Tonkin Gulf Resolution had been repealed, when the war was winding down. Avoiding the issue might then have seemed safest, institutionally, for the Court.

It remains to be seen whether American actions in Nicaragua—indistinguishable in principle from a "hot" war even without any contingents of U.S. troops there—will stand up under Court scrutiny. What the United States has been doing has been held by an international tribunal to be in violation of American treaty obligations, and that "law of the land" clause in Article VI would seemingly have some weight. A law that was prompted by the Vietnam action—the War Powers Resolution of 1973—has not yet been tested. It attempts to curtail free-wheeling executive use of military troops. Recent presidents have avoided complying with its efforts to enforce the Constitution's prescripts.

New Court history may begin in 1987–88. Questions thought to have been settled may be vulnerable to re-opening.

Affirmative action: During 1986, the Court thrice reaffirmed earlier rulings accepting remedial racial classifications, despite a Justice Department reversal of all pre-1981 positions. The verdict is that reparations can be directed or agreed upon for the massive deprivation that resulted from earlier, long-continued violations of the Constitution's guarantee of equal protection. The 1986 rulings have been reaffirmed twice in key cases involving blacks and women so far in 1987.

Privacy: The Ninth Amendment recognizes the possible existence of rights not specified in the Constitution. The Court enforced in 1965 the independent validity of the right to privacy, itself implicit in the First, Fourth, and Fifth Amendments. The idea of such a right was not new: it was mentioned in Court *dictum* even before Louis D. Brandeis launched his formal advocacy of what he called the "right to be left alone" in 1890. It was applied in relation to an obviously compelling area—sex—first in respect to the availability of contraception. A woman's freedom to choose whether to continue an unwanted pregnancy was affirmed as embraced in that right. However, responding to bitter controversy, the Court denied that the right to privacy guaranteed equal protection to women unable to pay for their own medical services. The Court may be weakening further, as shown by a doctrinally questionable ruling denying privacy protection to homosexuals.

Religious establishment: The First Amendment provides not merely for religious freedom, but for protection from government support to any sect or religion in general. Phases of this issue have almost ceaselessly been debated ever since the Court, in applying the First Amendment to the states as a result of the Fourteenth, upheld the complaint of parents who objected to a particular form of school prayer being composed by authorities. Confused rulings as to the extent to which schools that are organized privately and administered by religious bodies can receive state support have added to that debate. In the summer of 1985, Attorney General Edwin Meese seemed to suggest in an address decrying recent rulings on church-state relations that the Fourteenth Amendment's application of the Bill of Rights to the states should be undone as unsound.

Federalism updated: The dominant feature of twentieth-century constitutional activity has been the realization in legal fact of the transformation pithily described by Carl Sandburg: "Before the Civil War, the United States *were;* since the Civil War, and the Fourteenth Amendment, the United States *is. . . .*" Economically, that transformation had begun to take place with mid-nineteenth-century industrialization and railroad building; legally, it was deferred until the Fourteenth Amendment was revitalized as to human rights and full commerce regulatory power was set in place with the 1937–39 constitutional revolution. This regulatory control assumed new potential as industry and commerce attained dimensions unimagined by its drafters.

"Federalism" is the concept fundamental to that transformation. Historically and in contemporary debate, it can have as many superimposed colorations as there are political views being expressed. By definition, it means essentially no more than that the people within a large political entity have delegated administrative authority and responsibility to a single central body on the one hand, and to smaller, distinct local bodies on the other. The proportions of authority given to the central body and the local bodies can vary enormously. To say that "federalism is dead," or that there should be a "new federalism," can be misleading. Analytically, the only relevant inquiry is the proportion of the division.

Rivalry for "sovereignty" between the overall body and the component parts marked our pre-Civil War period. Ambiguity was the result of an unavoidable flaw in the unamended, original Constitution. It should have been resolved by the Civil War amendments. That it wasn't—that state freedom to ignore national standards of human rights survived—was tragic. The deferred realization of the amendments' meaning and power resulted in part from the desire to salvage the economic arrangement that slavery represented. In part it was the result of a good-faith belief in the virtues of decentralization. Present-day cases that reflect judicial ambivalence include the application of federal wage/hour laws to state employees—the Court has reversed itself twice in the last seventeen years on this issue. These cases are the result of *both* anti-centralizing viewpoints—reactionary and progressive.

"Progressive" is plainly the word for a new phase of constitutional law, following the shift in the Supreme Court to what two of its current members have called "too narrow and niggardly" readings of the rights amendments. State courts of last resort have in reasingly rejuvenated their own constitutions to impose high standards of rights-respecting behavior on their own local authorities. This century's revival of the Fourteenth and sister amendments, has made constitutional changes unnecessary in many states, where state judges educated by the revival act with more widsom and vision than the shrinking federal rights standards currently reveal.

TEACHING ACTIVITIES

FREEDOM OF SPEECH IN AMERICAN LIFE

Richard J. Morey

Introduction

The purpose of this activity is to illustrate the significance of freedom of speech in the United States. The lesson sheds light upon the role of speech and expression in any society, including the school community. The Supreme Court decision in *Gitlow v. New York* (1925) is the centerpiece of this lesson. Through study of this landmark case, students will gain an appreciation of the delicate balance between an individual's right to free speech and the government's need to protect itself from speech that is likely to risk the nation's security. Important to this lesson is the recognition that freedom of speech is not an absolute right, and that methods of achieving the balance between the private right and the public need are well-intentioned, but not foolproof.

During the First World War, the administration of President Wilson encouraged Americans to entertain a strong dislike for the German enemy. This effort helped to set the stage for the Red Scare of 1919 and 1920. In these postwar years, many Americans transferred their wartime antipathies to a new and more shadowy menace: world communism. Russia had fallen into the hands of the Bolsheviks, and radical socialist movements were growing in the countries of western Europe. Socialists and communists in the United States found themselves under increasing and unfriendly scrutiny from fearful American citizens.

Not long before the Red Scare, the New York state legislature had refused to seat some duly elected socialists, and in 1925 the Supreme Court heard arguments in the case of Benjamin Gitlow. Gitlow was a radical socialist, though not an anarchist. He had nonetheless been convicted under New York's 1902 Criminal Anarchy Act, which forbade advocating the overthrow of the government through forceful or violent means. This law had been passed in response to public outrage at the assassination of President McKinley in Buffalo in 1901.

Benjamin Gitlow had written and published 16,000 copies of "The Left Wing Manifesto," and had distributed several of these pamphlets. Gitlow, who considered himself a kind of revolutionary socialist, was the leader of a group called the Left Wing, which in this pamphlet was announcing its break with the regular Socialist Party.

Gitlow's angry publication was in large part an imitative borrowing from the 1848 *Communist Manifesto* of Marx and Engels. It called for the overthrow of the government by "*class action* of the proletariat *in any form* having as its objective the conquest of the power of the state." The "Left Wing Manifesto" further urged its readers to "organize . . . for the *coercion and suppression of the bourgeoisie,*" and concluded with this exhortation: "The Communist International calls the proletariat of the world to the final struggle!"

The Supreme Court, with Justice Edward Sanford writing for the majority, upheld Gitlow's conviction. Justice Oliver Wendell Holmes, the originator of the "clear and present danger" test of free speech, did not believe that the "Left Wing Manifesto" represented a genuine threat to the nation. Constitutional historians since have tended to agree with the dissenting opinion of Justice Holmes.

Procedure

1. Read the following quotation to the class. Do not identify its source until a few students have reacted to it.

   > Why should a government which believes it is doing what is right allow itself to be criticized? It would not allow opposition by lethal weapons. Ideas are much more fatal things than guns. . . .

2. Reveal that the quotation comes from a statement made by Lenin in Moscow in 1920. (This quotation will help to set the First Amendment guarantee of freedom of speech into context.)
3. Have students read the text of the First Amendment, pointing out that the historical purpose of the Bill of Rights was to protect personal liberties against government intrusion. (Teachers might ask students to take a few minutes to write a paragraph that begins, "Free speech is _____ ," or "Americans have free speech when _____ ." Students' responses will show that there is a range of opinion as to how much freedom can be tolerated.)
4. Ask students to enumerate ways in which free speech is a part of everyday American life. Encourage them to point out how many of their classes invite open discussion and conflicting points of view, and how public disagreements are seldom improper or illegal. Ask students to recall instances when leading public officials have been publicly criticized. (Examples might include Elie Wiesel's objections to President Reagan's planned visit to the Bitburg cemetery in Germany, made in the White House with the President seated next to him.)
5. Introduce the formulation devised by Justice Oliver Wendell Holmes for determining when personal freedom of speech must give way to the greater needs of society as a whole. Justice Holmes proposed his influential "clear and present danger" test for setting the limits of speech in an open society in his ruling in *Schenck v. U.S.* (1919). Developing his famous hypothetical situation, Holmes wrote:

   > But the character of every act depends upon the circumstances in which it is done. The most stringent protection of free speech would not protect a man in falsely shouting fire in a theatre and causing a panic. . . . The question in every case is whether the words are used in such circumstances and are of such a nature as to create a clear and present danger that they will bring about the substantive evils that Congress has a right to protect. . . .

6. Present the case of Benjamin Gitlow. Allow students to sample the rhetoric of Gitlow's "Left Wing Manifesto." Before letting students know the

Supreme Court's decision in the case, ask students if they think that the "Left Wing Manifesto" passes or fails the test proposed by Holmes.

7. Reveal the Supreme Court's decision, and direct students' attention to the following excerpts from Justice Edward Sanford's opinion:

> The Manifesto, plainly, is neither the statement of abstract doctrine nor, as suggested by [Gitlow's] counsel, mere prediction that industrial disturbances and revolutionary mass strikes will result spontaneously. . . . It advocates and urges in fervent language mass action which will foment . . . disturbances. . . . This is not the expression of philosophical abstraction, the mere prediction of future events: it is the language of direct incitement.

   Ask students to write a précis, or synopsis, of these excerpts, so that they will clearly understand how dangerous Justice Sanford believed Gitlow's writing to be.

8. Explain that Justice Holmes thought that Justice Sanford had applied the wrong test in reaching his decision. Give students a key portion of his dissent to examine:

> If what I think the correct test is applied, it is manifest that there was no present danger of an attempt to overthrow the government by force on the part of the admittedly small minority who shared the defendant's views. It is said [by Justice Sanford] that this Manifesto was more than a theory, that it was an incitement. Every idea is an incitement. It offers itself for belief, and, if believed, it is acted on unless some other belief outweighs it, or some failure of energy stifles the movement at its birth. The only difference between the expression of an opinion and an incitement in the narrow sense is the speaker's enthusiasm for the result. Eloquence may set fire to reason. But whatever may be thought of the redundant discourse before us, it had no chance of starting a present conflagration.

9. Ask students to explain the fallacy that Justice Holmes believed that he had discovered in Justice Sanford's reasoning. (Students should come away from this discussion with an understanding of the difficulty of reaching agreement upon what poses a danger that is both clear *and* present. Though Justices Sanford and Holmes agreed that Gitlow's pamphlet posed a *clear* danger, they sincerely disagreed upon the question of whether it posed a *present* danger.)

10. Tell students that constitutional historians have since tended to side with Justice Holmes and have generally agreed that Justice Sanford applied a "bad tendency" test, rather than the "clear and present danger" test. He reasoned that the pamphlet's *tending* to objectionable action was enough to condemn it—in other words, Justice Sanford saw a *probable,* rather than a *present,* danger in the "Left Wing Manifesto." By the late 1950s, the Supreme Court had rejected the Sanford interpretation and embraced the Holmes formulation of the meaning of clear and present danger.

11. In concluding this activity, bring to students' attention this remarkable passage that Justice Sanford very quietly tucked into his opinion:

> For present purposes we may and do assume that freedom of speech and of the press—which are protected by the 1st Amendment from abridgment by Congress—are among the fundamental personal rights and "liberties" protected by the due process clause of the 14th Amendment from impairment by the states. . . .

Emphasize the fact that, despite Gitlow's own misfortune in the outcome of his case, the Supreme Court did name freedom of speech as an essential right and has held it to be so ever since.

12. As follow-up activities, teachers can ask students to:

- Write about freedom of speech in their school. They can examine primary documents, such as the student handbook, student council guidelines, and so on. If they feel that there are too many restrictions, they should propose changes.
- Try to create useful clarifications of the "clear and present danger" test. In doing so, students should consider whether particular historical events since the time of Holmes call for modifications of his test in one direction or another.
- Examine other, more recent cases involving freedom of speech—in particular, *Dennis v. U.S.* (1951) and *Yates v. U.S.* (1957). *Tinker v. DesMoines* (1969) dealt with symbolic speech—the wearing of black armbands to symbolize antiwar views at the time of the Vietnam engagement.

Postscript: Students may wonder what happened to Benjamin Gitlow after he lost his appeal to the Supreme Court. He continued serving his five-year sentence in New York's prison at Sing Sing, until he was pardoned by Governor Al Smith later in 1925. He subsequently joined the Communist Party and twice served as its vice-presidential candidate. By the early 1950s, however, Benjamin Gitlow had become a passionate enemy of communism here and abroad.

BROWN v. BOARD OF EDUCATION: YOU BE THE JUDGE

Ronald Levitsky

Introduction

This study of the historic case of *Brown v. Board of Education* is designed to make students aware of the two impulses that perpetually motivate and influence the Supreme Court in its interpretations of the Constitution. The Court constantly responds to the pull of the past, preserving tradition and respecting precedent, at the same time that it is continually reacting to the pull of current events and social innovation. In this activity, students will examine the gradually evolving legal precedents that led up to *Brown v. Board of Education* and made it possible for the Court to rule that separating the members of different races, even with the intention of treating all segregated groups equally, necessarily and inherently creates inequalities which are unconstitutional. In the case of each precedent, students will see the pull of past and present circumstances.

Procedure

1. Guide students in reading and discussing Articles III and IV of the Constitution, as well as the Fourteenth Amendment.
2. Distribute Resource Sheets 1 and 2. As homework, students should read Resource Sheet 1 carefully and be able to explain how the Supreme Court's view of segregated schools changed over the years. They should also cut the quotations on Resource Sheet 2 into "index cards" and arrange them chronologically. (Teachers may wish to assign students the task of constructing a time-line entitled "The Supreme Court and Civil Rights.")
3. On the next day, divide the class into legal teams (three or four students per team). Assign one side of *Brown v. Board of Education* to each team, so that both the plaintiff (Brown) and the defendant (Board of Education) are represented by three or four teams.
4. Allow sufficient time for each team to prepare a list of the arguments in favor of its client. Each group may turn to the Constitution and Resource Sheets 1 and 2, which include precedent cases. Groups may also resort to imaginary witnesses likely to testify on behalf of their clients—e.g., a child psychologist for Brown, or the principal of a black high school for the Board of Education. Each team should arrange its arguments in order of importance and be ready to justify the order. The index cards from the second resource sheet can be arranged to support a team's arguments.
5. At the end of the allotted time, reconvene the class. Acting as moderator, call upon a team representing Brown, and write one of its arguments on the board. Ask the team to explain its reasoning. Then call upon one of the

Board of Education's teams for an opposing argument, write it on the board, and ask for an explanation. Repeat the process until every team has had an opportunity to respond and all arguments have been exhausted.

6. If time permits, see if the teams on each side of the case can reach a consensus as to which argument on behalf of their client is strongest.
7. "Transform" the entire class into the Supreme Court. Review the arguments on the board. Then try to establish which side has the stronger case. Emphasize the Constitution and precedent cases as evidence; refer to the "index cards" of Resource Sheet 2. Take a vote. (A secret ballot might ensure that each student votes his or her conscience.)
8. As a follow-up activity, teachers may wish to assign or discuss one or more of these questions:
   - Compare the *Plessy* decision to the decision in *Brown* with regard to the concept of federalism.
   - Why do you think that the Supreme Court overturned *Plessy?* Considering Justice Harlan's minority opinion (index card #7), discuss how minority opinions can sometimes lead to majority decisions.
   - Because the Constitution was written two hundred years ago, is it justifiable—even necessary—for the Supreme Court's interpretation of it to change with the times?

RESOURCE SHEET 1
HISTORICAL BACKGROUND OF *BROWN v. BOARD OF EDUCATION*

The United States Supreme Court preserves our nation's traditions at the same time that it adjusts to social change. Both tradition and change played important roles in the court's famous decision in *Brown v. Board of Education of Topeka, Kansas.* This case, dealing with segregation in the public schools, demonstrates the Constitution as a living document, whose meaning is continually studied and interpreted by the highest court of the land.

Following the Civil War, the Thirteenth, Fourteenth, and Fifteenth Amendments to the Constitution outlawed slavery, granted citizenship with full privileges and immunities to all persons born or naturalized in the United States, and protected the right of all citizens to vote, regardless of race, color, or previous status as slaves. Despite these amendments, many communities throughout the United States established separate facilities for blacks and whites, such as segregated restaurants, hotels, and even drinking fountains.

In 1896, Homer Plessy, who was one-eighth Negro, refused to leave a "whites-only" railway car, thus defying a Louisiana law establishing separate, but equal railway cars for blacks and whites. Arrested for breaking the law, Plessy appealed to the Supreme Court. He argued that his rights as a citizen under the Fourteenth Amendment were denied. The Court ruled that state laws could separate the races, as long as the separate facilities were of equal quality. *Plessy v. Ferguson* became an important "precedent"—a decision that would influence later judicial opinions on segregation.

The "separate but equal" doctrine was also applied to education. It was not uncommon for a school district to have black and white school systems operating side by side. Not only was this discriminatory duplication of facilities held to be constitutional, but much less sophisticated forms of racial discrimination in education were held to be constitutional, as well. In *Cumming v. Richmond County Board of Education* (1899), the Supreme Court allowed a school board to discontinue its black high school, for financial reasons, while continuing to operate its white high school. And in *Gong Lum v. Rice* (1927), the Supreme Court decided that Mississippi could require a nine-year-old Chinese girl to attend a black school, even though it was inferior to the white one.

However, as black people struggled for equality, the Supreme Court's interpretation of the Constitution slowly began to change. In the case of *Missouri ex rel. Gaines v. Canada* (1938), Lloyd Gaines, a black man of 25, wanted to attend the University of Missouri Law School, which was for whites only. Because there was no separate black law school in the state, Missouri had offered to pay any extra tuition expenses for Gaines to attend a non-segregated law school in a neighboring state, while Missouri would begin building a separate black law school. Gaines refused and demanded to enter the University of Missouri. The Supreme Court supported him, ruling that the white law school at the University of Missouri had to accept him, since Missouri did not have a separate black law school of its own. The Court finally supported the idea that segregated schools really had to be equal.

Two other cases, both decided in 1950, continued to change the way in which the Supreme Court viewed school segregation—especially at the university level. In *Sweatt v. Painter,* the Court ruled that the University of Texas had to admit Sweatt, a black man, to its all-white law school, even though there was a separate black law school in the state, because the black school was inferior in such "intangible" qualities as prestige and reputation of faculty.

George McLaurin, a black man of 68, applied to and was admitted by the University of Oklahoma to study for a doctorate in education. Oklahoma acknowledged that it had no adequate black school and allowed black students to attend its all-white university, but on a segregated basis. McLaurin was made to sit at a desk by himself outside the regular classroom, eat by himself in an alcove in the cafeteria, and study alone behind a stack of newspapers in the library. In *McLaurin v. Oklahoma State Regents,* the Supreme Court found these restrictions based on segregation to be unconstitutional, because McLaurin's ability to get an education was unfairly restricted.

These decisions seemed to indicate that universities could not be segregated, because they really could not be equal. But what about the millions of children in elementary and high schools—could they still be kept in segregated schools? This question was decided in five court cases in 1954, the most famous of which was *Brown v. Board of Education of Topeka, Kansas.*

Mr. Oliver Brown did not want his 11-year-old daughter to walk across railroad tracks a mile to the black school, when the white school was less than half a mile away. Although the board of education made a strong argument that its black and white schools were physically equal, the Supreme Court ruled in favor of Brown on the key question that had divided many of America's schools since the Civil War—that even if the physical facilities were equal, the very fact of segregation deprived black children of an equal education.

Thus, nearly sixty years later, the Supreme Court reversed itself and held that *Plessy v. Ferguson* was no longer valid. Schools could no longer be segregated.

RESOURCE SHEET 2
THE SUPREME COURT AND CIVIL RIGHTS

1. *Brown v. Board of Education* (1954) "We must look . . . to the effect of segregation itself on public education. . . . To separate them [blacks] from others of similar age and qualifications solely because of their race generates a feeling of inferiority as to their status in the community that may affect their hearts and minds in a way unlikely ever to be undone. . . . Separate educational facilities are inherently unequal."	**2. *Cumming v. Richmond County Board of Education* (1899)** ". . . the education of people in schools maintained by state taxation is a matter belonging to the respective states, and any interference on the part of Federal authority with the management of such schools cannot be justified except in the case of a clear and unmistakable disregard of rights secured by the supreme law of the land. We have here no such case to be determined."
3. *Gong Lum v. Rice* (1927) ". . . we think that it is the same question that has been many times decided to be within the constitutional power of the state legislature to settle, without intervention of the federal courts. . . ."	**4. *McLaurin v. Oklahoma State Regents* (1950)** "The result [of restrictions] is that appellant [McLaurin] is handicapped in his pursuit of effective graduate instruction. Appellant, having been admitted to a state-supported graduate school, must receive the same treatment at the hands of the state as students of other races."
5. *Missouri ex rel. Gaines v. Canada* (1938) "It was as an individual that he [Gaines] was entitled to the equal protection of the laws, and the State was bound to furnish him within its borders facilities for legal education substantially equal to those which the State there afforded for persons of the white race, whether or not other Negroes sought the same opportunity."	**6. *Plessy v. Ferguson* (1896)—majority opinion** "Laws permitting and even requiring their [black and white] separation in places where they are liable to be brought into contact do not necessarily imply the inferiority of either race to the other. . . . If one race be inferior to the other socially, the Constitution of the United States cannot put them upon the same plane."
7. *Plessy v. Ferguson* (1896)—minority opinion (Justice Harlan) "Our Constitution is color-blind, and neither knows nor tolerates classes among citizens. In respect of civil rights, all citizens are equal before the law. . . . The destinies of the two races in this country are indissolubly linked together, and the interests of both require that the common government of all shall not permit the seeds of race hate to be planted under the sanction of law."	**8. *Sweatt v. Painter* (1950)** ". . . the University of Texas Law School possesses to a far greater degree those qualities which are incapable of objective measurement but which make for greatness in a law school. . . . With such a substantial and significant segment of society [i.e., blacks] excluded, we cannot conclude that the education offered petitioner [at a separate black law school] is substantially equal to that which he would receive if admitted to the University of Texas Law School."

UNITED STATES v. NIXON: THE SCOPE OF EXECUTIVE PRIVILEGE

Gordon Mixdorf

Introduction

This activity focuses on the historical and constitutional development of the concept of executive privilege. It enables students to explore the historical precedents for executive privilege and to decide whether or not Richard Nixon's refusal to surrender the Watergate tapes was constitutional.

The Watergate affair serves as a major example of presidential abuse of power in the twentieth century. Nixon's assertion of executive privilege to prevent Congress and the courts from gaining access to his tapes of conversations in the Oval Office seriously challenged the concept of a balance of power among the three branches of the federal government. The decision of the Supreme Court in 1974 to limit executive privilege was important in maintaining a balance and separation of powers. The Court acknowledged a constitutional basis for executive privilege and then focused upon the relationship of executive privilege to the judicial process, ruling that a claim of executive privilege does not make a president immune from judicial process under all circumstances.

Procedure

1. Discuss the background of Watergate, the revelation of the existence of the tapes, Nixon's attempts to withhold them from the investigation, and Circuit Court Judge John Sirica's order to surrender them, which led Nixon to appeal to the Supreme Court.
2. Divide the class into groups of no more than five students. Each group will act as a miniature Supreme Court, ruling in the case of *United States v. Nixon.* Student justices should be reminded that their decision will serve as a precedent for future decisions. Therefore, they should be guided by general principles and past precedents, at the same time that they examine the specific case at hand.
3. Give each group a copy of the information sheet, "Historical and Legal Precedents for Executive Privilege," and a copy of the "Student Decision Sheet."
4. When the groups have arrived at their decisions, ask each group to present its opinion and its reasoning.
5. Distribute and discuss the excerpts from the actual decision of the Supreme Court in *United States v. Nixon.* Analyze differences between student decisions and the actual decision. The discussion should touch upon the impact and influence of criticism of Nixon's behavior in the media, the

convictions of White House officials, and the growing sentiment for impeachment in the House of Representatives.

HISTORICAL AND LEGAL PRECEDENTS FOR EXECUTIVE PRIVILEGE

• President Washington refused to allow the House of Representatives to see papers concerning the Jay Treaty, declaring that the House lacked constitutional power to demand documents related to treaties. He acknowledged the Senate's right of access to the material, however.

• Chief Justice Marshall ruled in *Marbury v. Madison* that, "By the Constitution of the United States, the president is invested with certain important political powers, in the exercise of which he is to use his own discretion, and is accountable only to his country in his political character and to his own conscience."

However, Marshall saw that there were limits—especially if the legal rights of a citizen were involved. Therefore, he hints at, but does not directly discuss, a separation of executive and judicial control over access to information.

• In the 1807 trial of Aaron Burr for treason, Thomas Jefferson supplied information to the House of Representatives about the controversy. The House had requested letters in Jefferson's possession. He turned over the letters, but deleted names that appeared in them.

Chief Justice Marshall, who presided at the trial, recognized a limited privilege of the president to protect state secrets, but said that the court would weigh the need for secrecy against the needs of the accused.

• President Andrew Jackson rejected a request by the Senate in 1835 for a list of charges against Surveyor-General Fitz in an investigation of fraudulent land sales.

• Presidents Tyler, Polk, and Pierce all withheld information demanded by Congress.

In the twentieth century:

• The Supreme Court acknowledged in *Boske v. Comingore* (1900) and *U.S. ex rel. Touhy v. Ragan, Warden, et al.* (1951) that heads of executive departments can raise claims of executive privilege with respect to court orders for records of the department of the testimony of employees.

• In *McGrain v. Daugherty* (1927), the Supreme Court ruled that executive privilege does not protect the executive branch from legitimate legislative investigation, upholding the right of the Senate to investigate the Attorney General's failure to prosecute key figures in the Teapot Dome scandal.

• In *Chicago and Southern Airlines v. Waterman S.S. Co.* (1948), the Court acknowledged that there are areas of executive power—military and national security matters, in particular—where the president might properly refuse to disclose all facts relative to a decision: "The President, both as Commander-in-Chief and as the Nation's organ for foreign affairs, has available services whose reports neither are nor ought to be published to the world. . . ."

• In *U.S. v. Reynolds* (1953), the Court ruled that it could decide on a case-by-case basis whether or not the executive privilege had been appropriately applied in withholding information to protect military or national security secrets: "In each case, the showing of necessity . . . will determine how far the court should probe in satisfying itself that the occasion for invoking the privilege is appropriate."

• In 1954, President Eisenhower wrote a letter to the Secretary of Defense, Charles Wilson, directing him to instruct people under him not to testify before Senator Joseph McCarthy's Army Hearings. For the next seven years, Eisenhower's letter was the major authority cited for the "executive privilege" to refuse to provide information to Congress.

• In 1962, President Kennedy refused a special Senate subcommittee's request that he identify individuals assigned to edit speeches for military leaders, saying that ". . . each case must be judged on its own merits . . . executive privilege can be invoked only by the President and will not be used without specific Presidential approval. . . ."

• In 1965, President Johnson declared that ". . . the claim of executive privilege will continue to be made only by the President. . . ."

• In a 1971 memorandum to heads of all executive departments and agencies, President Nixon wrote that ". . . executive privilege will not be used without specific Presidential approval. . . ." (In 1973, however, some executive branch officials during the Nixon administration did claim "executive privilege" without presidential approval.)

STUDENT DECISION SHEET

Questions about the controversy:

1. What is the nature of executive privilege?
2. Did President Nixon meet the requirements to claim executive privilege?
3. Is there such a thing as "absolute" executive privilege?

Decision choices:

1. Nixon should be ordered to turn over the tapes.
2. The President's executive privilege is absolute and cannot be abridged by the Court through the subpoena process. Therefore, Nixon does not have to turn over the tapes.

In writing your decision, resolve the following questions:

1. How important is the concept of checks and balances?
2. How important is the concept of executive privilege?
3. To what extent should executive privilege be respected or restricted?

Upon completion of your decision and the summation of arguments, select one of the group to present your decision.

UNITED STATES v. NIXON
July 24, 1974

The Supreme Court unanimously rejected Nixon's claim of privilege. Speaking for a unanimous Court, Chief Justice Warren Burger discussed the derivation of executive privilege:

> Whatever the nature of the privilege of confidentiality of presidential communications in the exercise of Art. II powers the *privilege can be said to derive from the supremacy of each branch within its own assigned area of constitutional duties.* Certain powers and privileges flow from the nature of the enumerated powers; the protection of the

confidentiality of presidential communications has similiar constitutional underpinnings.

The Court then observed that:

> . . . *neither* the doctrine of separation of powers, nor the need for confidentiality of high level communications, without more, *can sustain an absolute, unqualified presidential privilege of immunity from judicial process under all circumstances.* . . . The impediment that an *absolute, unqualified privilege* would place in the way of the primary constitutional duty of the Judicial Branch to do justice in criminal prosecutions would *plainly confict with the function of the courts under Art. III.* In designing the structure of our Government and dividing and allocating the sovereign power among three coequal branches, the Framers of the Constitution sought to provide a comprehensive system, but the *separate powers were not intended to operate with absolute independence.* . . .
>
> To read the Art. II powers of the President as providing an absolute privilege as against a subpoena essential to enforcement of criminal statutes on no more than a generalized claim of the public interest in confidentiality of nonmilitary and nondiplomatic discussions would upset the constitutional balance of "a workable government" and gravely impair the role of the courts under Art. III. . . .

In rejecting this particular claim of privilege, however, the Court for the first time acknowledged a constitutional basis for executive privilege:

> A President and those who assist him must be freed to explore alternatives in the process of shaping policies and making decisions and to do so in a way many would be unwilling to express except privately. These are the considerations justifying a presumptive privilege for presidential communications. The privilege is fundamental to the operation of government and inextricably rooted in the separation of powers under the Constitution. . . .
>
> Nowhere in the Constitution . . . is there any explicit reference to a privilege of confidentiality, yet to the extent this interest relates to the effective discharge of a President's powers, it is constitutionally based. . . .

In this case the *claim of an absolute privilege failed when weighed against the requirements of evidence in a criminal proceeding.* Burger observed:

> No case of the Court . . . has extended this high degree of deference to a President's generalized interest in confidentiality. . . .
>
> In this case we must weigh the importance of the general privilege of confidentiality of presidential communications in performance of his responsibilities against the inroads of such a privilege on the fair administration of criminal justice. The interest in preserving confidentiality is weighty indeed and entitled to great respect. However we cannot conclude that advisers will be moved to temper the candor of their remarks by the infrequent occasions of disclosure because of the possibility that such conversations will be called for in the context of a criminal prosecution . . .
>
> A President's acknowledged need for confidentiality in the communications of his office is general in nature, whereas the constitutional need for production of relevant evidence in a criminal proceeding is specific and central to the fair adjudication of a particular criminal case in the administration of justice. Without access to specific facts a criminal prosecution may be totally frustrated. The President's broad interest in confidentiality of communications will not be vitiated by disclosure of a limited number of conversations preliminarily shown to have some bearing on the pending criminal cases.
>
> We conclude that when the ground for asserting privilege as to subpoened materials sought for use in a criminal trial is based only on the generalized interest in confidentiality, it cannot prevail over the fundamental demands of due process of law in the fair administration of criminal justice. The generalized assertion of privilege must yield to the demonstrated, specific need for evidence in a pending criminal trial. . . .

(Excerpted from Congressional Quarterly, *Guide to the U.S. Supreme Court,* 1979, pp. 229–234.)

TRACKING THE EQUAL RIGHTS AMENDMENT THROUGH THE AMENDMENT PROCESS

Fay Metcalf and Jill Louise Fernandez

Introduction

The purpose of this activity is to help students to understand the process established by the framers and specified in Article V for amending the Constitution. Students will learn the mechanics of this process by studying the recent unsuccessful effort to add an "Equal Rights Amendment" to the Constitution. By focusing on the ERA, the activity will demonstrate the impediments to a proposed amendment that has a great deal of support, yet falls short of having the support of a large majority of the nation's legislators.

The first resource sheet for this activity explains the amendment process and is intended to facilitate study of Article V. The second resource sheet chronicles the efforts to propose and ratify the Equal Rights Amendment. This case history amply illustrates the hurdles that the amendment process sets in the path of any prospective amendment. It also highlights the social controversy that sharply divided public opinion about this amendment. At the same time, students will see that Americans fundamentally are not eager to change the Constitution—a document that has so clearly withstood the test of time.

Procedure

1. Distribute the first resource sheet, "Amending the Constitution," which shows the amendment process, and read and discuss Article V of the Constitution.
2. Distribute the second resource sheet, "The Equal Rights Amendment: Is it Resting in Peace?" Ask students to read it silently or aloud.
3. Direct students to prepare a position statement on either (a) the processes used in the case of this amendment, or (b) the merits of this amendment.
4. Poll students as to their positions, and have them use their statements as the basis for a panel discussion or classroom debate. In writing position statements, students should ask themselves:
   - What social values were in conflict in the controversy over the ERA?
   - Were the concerns expressed by ERA opponents legitimate ones?
   - What tactics could ERA supporters use most effectively in a new effort to get the bill passed? Should the amendment be rewritten before being resubmitted?
   - What tactics could opponents use most effectively in fending off any new attempt?

In addition, students taking a position on the processes used in the case of the Equal Rights Amendment might research the circumstances surrounding the proposal and ratification of the Civil Rights Amendment of 1964 (banning poll taxes in federal elections). They could compare and contrast the content of the 1964 amendment and the ERA, and the ratification process.

If students desire more information, the *Reader's Guide to Periodical Literature* cites dozens of articles in magazines that are usually found in school libraries.

AMENDING THE CONSTITUTION

The framers of the Constitution realized that, if their work were to last, they would have to provide a means that would permit the document to adapt to changes in society. Article V explains how the Constitution can be amended, or changed. Amending the document involves an elaborate process. The chart below shows how the Constitution may be amended.

The Amending Process

Methods of Proposing Amendments

By Congress with two-thirds vote of both houses

By National Constitutional Convention called by Congress at the request of two-thirds of the state legislatures

Methods of Ratification

By Constitutional Conventions in three-fourths of the states

By Legislatures in three-fourths of the states

Note that the states wield a great deal of power in the amendment process. Article V establishes two methods of proposing amendments and two methods of ratifying them. One method makes the states instrumental in proposing an amendment. Both methods of ratification make the states, rather than the federal government, the principal actors, thus giving the states the final voice in the amendment process.

Note also that the Constitution makes it more difficult to ratify an amendment than to propose one, in terms of the majorities required. This reflects the fact that the framers regarded ratifying as a more serious business than proposing an amendment.

The framers devised this process to safeguard the Constitution from being amended too hastily or for insignificant or harmful reasons.

THE EQUAL RIGHTS AMENDMENT: IS IT RESTING IN PEACE?

Origins of the ERA

The concept of a constitutional amendment guaranteeing equality of rights to all individuals regardless of sex was formally proposed in 1923 by Alice Paul, founder of the National Women's Party. The "Equal Rights Amendment" (ERA), as this bill became known, was introduced into Congress that same year. Its wording was concise. In its entirety, it read:

The Equal Rights Amendment
Section 1.
Equality of rights under the law shall not be denied or abridged by the United States or by any State on account of sex.
Section 2.
The Congress shall have the power to enforce, by appropriate legislation, the provision of this Article.
Section 3.
This amendment shall take effect two years after the date of ratification.

No effort was made to bring up the Equal Rights Amendment for discussion until 1967, when it was formally endorsed and publicized by the National Organization of Women. In 1972, Congress passed the ERA bill and set a seven-year deadline for completion of the ratification process. By the end of that year, 22 states had ratified the amendment. Then the momentum declined, however.

The long drive for ratification

In several states, opponents of the amendment waged a steady campaign against the ERA. Supporters, worried that they would not meet the seven-year deadline, lobbied for more time. Congress agreed to extend the ratification period for an additional three years and set a new deadline of June 30, 1982.

Then, in March of 1979, in an unprecedented move, five states voted to overturn their previous ratifications. Questions about the legality of rescinding ratification were resolved in December 1981, when U.S. District Court Judge Marion Callister ruled that states do indeed have the right to rescind passage of constitutional amendments. He also ruled that Congress had violated the Constitution by granting the three-year extension in 1979. These actions were major setbacks to ERA supporters.

With the final 1982 deadline approaching, lobbying increased in the undecided states, with efforts focusing on five key states: North Carolina, Missouri, Illinois, Oklahoma, and Florida. These efforts on behalf of the Equal Rights Amendment were unsuccessful in persuading legislators in these states, however, and on June 30, 1982, the drive for ratification of the ERA failed.

Attempts to resuscitate the ERA

Supporters of the ERA did not rest. On July 14, 1982, bills were introduced in both houses of Congress to submit the ERA once again to the states for ratification. At first, this second campaign seemed certain to succeed. House Speaker Thomas O'Neill (D-MA) called the ERA a top priority of the ninety-eighth Congress, and the bill was introduced with 221 cosponsors.

In May 1983, however, events at a meeting of the Senate Judiciary Committee's Subcommittee on the Constitution foreshadowed the bill's second failure. The chairman, Orrin Hatch (R-UT), had made no secret of his opposition to the amendment and his intent to orchestrate a crusade to defeat it. With Rex Lee, the U.S. Solicitor General, Hatch had written a book attacking the Equal Rights Amendment. The two men claimed that its wording was so unclear that no one had the slightest idea of what the amendment really meant.

To disprove Hatch's contention, ERA supporters marshalled arguments based on the recent legal gains made by women in states that had passed equal rights legislation. Plans went awry, however, when one of the bill's chief sponsors, Senator Paul Tsongas, appeared before the subcommittee. Tsongas did not expect and was unprepared for the several hours of probing questions to which Senator Hatch subjected him. His vague answers added fuel to the anti-ERA argument that the bill lacked clarity.

Failure to win a second chance

ERA opponents had now discovered a strategy by which to kill the amendment in the House of Representatives. They began immediately to exploit the general wording of the bill, proposing dozens of amendments to it that dealt with such volatile issues as abortion, the draft, marriage between homosexuals, and unisex toilets. These so-called "clarifying" amendments succeeded in linking some highly controversial issues to the Equal Rights Amendment.

Thus, supporters of the ERA found themselves embroiled in unanticipated controversy, and, in addition, they were unexpectedly pressed for time. An early congressional recess in mid-November gave supporters little time to get a vote in the House by the end of the year.

To head off the "clarification" strategy of the ERA opponents and ensure a vote before the congressional session ended, Speaker O'Neill and the two chief House sponsors of the bill, Don Edwards (D-CA) and Pat Schroeder (D-CO), decided to bring up the Equal Rights Amendment for an immediate vote under a special parliamentary procedure. This procedure limited debate on the bill to forty minutes and allowed no amendments to the original wording. The voting was conducted, and the Equal Rights Amendment fell just six votes short of the required two-thirds majority. To ERA supporters, the biggest surprise was that 14 of the original 245 cosponsors of the ERA had voted against the amendment.

The future of the ERA

Many supporters of the Equal Rights Amendment claim that this bill has not died. There are plans to reintroduce it in Congress at some future time. Supporters believe that the debate over the ERA has brought to light many of the issues and values at stake. They see two key areas of concern—the ERA's potential effects on a woman's right to terminate a pregnancy through abortion and on a woman's responsibility to serve in the military. Other areas in which the Equal Rights Amendment could have an impact include the role of women in the family, in the work place, and in the political arena.

It is unlikely that we have seen the last of the Equal Rights Amendment. As women become increasingly active in politics, this issue is likely to receive more and more attention and support. There are many issues involved in this debate, and a great deal of discussion will be necessary before they are resolved and the bill is either passed or finally laid to rest.

Part IV

Bibliography

CHAPTER 5

AN ANNOTATED BIBLIOGRAPHY

James J. Pyne and Mary K. Bonsteel Tachau

The literature on the Constitution is so extensive that it has taken others volumes simply to list it. This bibliography is a good deal more modest. The titles chosen constitute a very small sample of readily available, useful, and readable literature. The list of general surveys includes works whose breadth conveys something of the sweep of American constitutional development. A number of period studies concentrate on shorter time spans or specific subjects to sharpen the focus of the historical context in which constitutional development has occurred. The case studies provide greater depth on key constitutional developments and controversies. Collections of documents and sources are included to provide teachers with raw materials for their instruction on constitutional questions. They will also facilitate student research on constitutional themes and cases. The bibliographical guides will enable students and teachers alike to pursue particular interests. The annotation for each entry summarizes content, identifies major threads in the author's analysis or narrative, points out special features which may prove useful to teachers or students, and suggests who may profit from its use, and how.

GENERAL SURVEYS

Berry, Mary F. *Black Resistance/White Law: A History of Constitutional Racism in America.* Englewood Cliffs, New Jersey: Prentice-Hall, Inc., 1971.

Berry demonstrates that government reaction to racial violence and black rebellion between 1789 and 1970 was slow and uneven until they presented a great threat to whites. The federal government adopted a policy of noninterference unless states were unable to ward off black attacks on whites or their property. From the ratification of the Constitution until the Civil War, the central government readily used force to prevent black revolt, but did not oppose actions intended to suppress abolitionist activity. Moreover, it ignored or approved "on constitutional grounds" disorderly acts aimed at blacks. After 1865, federal and local law enforcement agencies usually disregarded white violence against blacks, pleading lack of jurisdiction under the Constitution. Only infrequently and rarely with success did the federal government use its constitutional power to protect blacks from whites. Berry concludes that this represented a lack of will rather than a lack of statutory or constitutional authority to intervene.

This is a superb source of information on racism justified by the Constitution. The manifestations of this racism ranged from campaigns against fugitive slaves to the suppression of racial violence in cities during the 1960s. Berry shows how the law and its constitutional base were used as a legal foundation for repressing a whole race of people, instead of a sacred foundation upon which freedom rests.

Flexner, Eleanor. *A Century of Struggle: The Woman's Rights Movement in the United States.* New York: Athenum, 1968.

This book is a study of the women's rights movement from its origins to 1920, with a special emphasis on the origins and development of the fight for women's suffrage. Flexner begins with a brief description of the position of women and their first efforts at organization in the years before the Civil War. The first burst of enthusiasm for suffrage was associated with the broad reforming impulse of the time, and particularly with abolition. The second section deals with the divisive dilemma that the women's suffrage movement confronted during Reconstruction: whether to support black suffrage at the expense of women's rights, or, instead, to risk political repercussions by insisting on universal suffrage. Flexner devotes the last third of the book to the crucial period from the unification of the suffrage movement after 1880 to its culmination in the ratification of the Nineteenth Amendment.

Teachers can use Flexner's study to bring a feminist perspective to a general survey course at points where constitutional rights and amendments surface as issues. It is especially useful in connection with the political controversies surrounding the Fourteenth, Fifteenth, and Nineteenth Amendments. Easy to read and filled with colorful portraits of women, it can be used profitably by students at most levels.

Friedman, Leon, and Fred L. Israel, compilers. *The Justices of the United States Supreme Court: Their Lives and Major Opinions.* Five volumes. New York: Chelsea House Publishers, 1980.

Friedman and Israel have compiled biographical essays on and selected opinions rendered by all United States Supreme Court justices. The work represents the efforts of more than forty contributors. Although the study of constitutional issues usually ignores the human qualities of the justices who decide them, the combined effect of these essays is to raise justices from obscurity—as the compilers proclaim, "to rescue the Court from the limbo of impersonality." Each essay includes sample opinions reflecting the jurisprudence of the justice in question.

These volumes are especially good for students and teachers investigating the lives and influence of specific justices or cases. More enterprising students can compare the views of different justices on the same cases. The entries on James Wilson, James Iredell, and John Blair, Jr., for example, all focus on their respective roles in *Chisholm v. Georgia* (1795). Students may thus study a single case from the perspective of different justices. The set invites comparison of justices over time, too, in order to trace the evolution of particular constitutional themes or interpretations from one era to another. There are also bibliographic references on each justice. The field of judicial biography has become increasingly important and popular, and the papers of many justices have been published. This collection may encourage students to undertake further investigation in this burgeoning field.

Hutson, James H. "The Creation of the Constitution: Scholarship at a Standstill." *Reviews in American History,* vol. 12 (December, 1984), 463–477.

"Historiography on the writing of the Constitution," Hutson concludes, "furnishes a vivid example of how contemporary events can influence the writing of history." Following ratification, the Founding Fathers were described as saviors who secured the nation from chaos. But from the abolitionists through the progressives and beyond, interpretations of the Constitution were controlled by its detractors—often partisans of reform frustrated by the Supreme Court's interpretation of the Constitution. Since the 1950s, with the Court's use of the Constitution as an instrument of democracy rather than as an obstacle to reform, historians have largely controlled interpretation. Yet, despite the dismantling of the Beard thesis, the result, Hutson laments, has been "a scholarly free-for-all." As successive interpretations have been found "untenable" by their inevitable critics, Hutson concludes that "the more these problems are studied, the more intractable they seem to become." Indeed, scholars have spoken in "such a Babel of voices" that our understanding of the Constitution seems to Hutson as imperfect now as it was when first written.

At once a crisp survey of the literature and a provocative criticism of historians, this valuable essay should be used with care by teachers. Hutson describes changing views clearly and reminds us how contemporary attitudes affect historical interpretation. But unless students are prepared for the prevalent disagreement among historians, they may very well abandon their efforts in despair.

Kelly, Alfred H., Winfred A. Harbison, and Herman Belz. *The American Constitution: Its Origins and Development.* Sixth edition. New York: W. W. Norton, 1983.

First published by Kelly and Harbison in 1948, this is the standard work in American constitutional history—as a reference tool, a text, and the best single-volume account of the American constitutional experience. This latest edition prepared by Belz claims to be a "substantially new book" which reflects "a thorough and comprehensive revision of both narrative and interpretation." Earlier editions focused on the centralization of power and increased government activism, but Belz mirrors current skepticism about the capacity of a centralized bureaucracy to fulfill ideals of liberty, equality, and democratic self-government. The thirty-three chapters are arranged chronologically to connect emerging constitutional themes to the historical context in which they appeared. Included are recent additions on the Watergate era and the crisis of the modern presidency, the Burger Court and contemporary constitutional law, and an epilogue on American constitutionalism in the 1980s.

Students and teachers will find this survey nearly indispensable. Teachers can use individual chapters to help infuse constitutional perspectives into their survey courses on virtually any topic under consideration. Students engaged in research on constitutional themes, cases, or topics will find this new edition by Belz the essential first step in the process. In addition to a handy table of cases, Belz has provided a magnificent seventy-five-page bibliography containing an incredible wealth and variety of sources.

McCloskey, Robert G. *The American Supreme Court*. Chicago: University of Chicago Press, 1972. The Chicago History of American Civilization.

McCloskey's brief and very readable treatment of the Court emphasizes the uses to which it has applied its power of judicial review. He traces the evolution of the concept from its earliest applications by Marshall and Taney, through the Gilded Age and the emergence of a welfare state, to the Court's handling of free speech and racial questions in the years after World War II. He describes the Court as an agent in the governing process "with a mind and a will and an influence of its own," as a "secular papacy," and as the repository of the nation's "political conscience." Paradoxically, the Court has actually "ruled more" when it has tried to "rule less." Its greatest difficulties, on the other hand, have come when the Court tried to dominate. The Court's historical problem, therefore, has been to decide when to intervene and to define the limits of judicial review.

McCloskey's survey was first published in 1960. In this edition he modifies his earlier views on judicial restraint. The survey is a superb introduction to the history of the Court and judicial review. Each chapter is an interpretive essay on one phase of the Court's history. Chapters may be used selectively to enhance a general survey course with a constitutional perspective, but most students will profit from a study of the whole book.

Peltason, Jack W., and Edward S. Corwin. *Understanding the Constitution*. Sixth edition. Hinsdale, Illinois: Dryden Press, 1973.

In this brief book, Peltason revises the work completed with Corwin and first published in 1949. Working from the premise that the Constitution is not self-explanatory, the book aims to make it understandable by "setting forth the main features of the Constitution and the practical significance of its most important provisions as they are construed and applied today." Each section of the Constitution is treated in non-technical language. The authors provide numerous references to key court cases throughout the volume. An introductory essay discusses the background of the Constitution. It explains the Declaration of Independence, the Articles of Confederation, the movement to strengthen the central government, and the Constitutional Convention. A second essay centers on basic principles of the Constitution such as federalism, separation of powers, and checks and balances.

This superb introduction to the Constitution is aimed at a general audience. Teachers can use it to help explain constitutional principles and specific clauses. Its greatest use will be for students, however, because it will help them to understand what the Constitution means and to appreciate the meaning of the provisions they are asked to study in the context of substantive controversies. *Understanding the Constitution* is a convenient, easy-to-use reference tool which will be valuable to students at most levels.

Washburn, Wilcomb E. *Red Man's Land/White Man's Law: A Study of the Past and Present Status of the American Indian.* New York: Charles Scribner and Sons, 1971.

Washburn's purpose is to describe "the process by which the Indian moved from sovereign to ward to citizen." Concerned primarily with the status of native Americans in the United States, Washburn details the history of the legal steps involved in the imposition of alien political authority upon the Native Americans which eroded their independence. In the first of four sections, the author deals with classical and Christian assumptions which conditioned Europeans' relations with the Indians they encountered in their conquest of the New World. The second section is a historical survey of the following three centuries and the corresponding evolution of attitudes concerning Indian status. The last two sections focus on the contemporary status of the Indian in light of current law and policy.

Washburn's overview of the relationship between Indians and the law will be helpful to teachers trying to include a Native American perspective in their survey courses. Students will find a twenty-page section on constitutional rights especially valuable. It concerns the dilemma of extending white civil rights to Indian cultures if they assault traditional native values. Washburn's emphasis in this section is on the Indian Constitutional Rights Act of 1968—a law criticized for imposing procedures on Indians which tended to "eliminate traditional ways of attaining the basic objectives of justice and equity."

White, G. Edward. *The American Judicial Tradition: Profiles of Leading American Judges.* New York: Oxford University Press, 1976.

In this set of biographical essays, White argues that the American judicial tradition was created during Marshall's tenure and largely through his efforts. This tradition consists of three elements: judicial independence checked mainly by "internalized constraints" such as those imposed by the Constitution; a sensitivity to political currents which holds the courts aloof from partisan politics but enables them to be an "active and weighty" political force; and "a recurrent trade-off" between the power of the judge and restraints on the judiciary. The first eight chapters detail the "oracular theory," according to which nineteenth-century judges "found" the law and "mechanically applied existing rules to new situations" without affecting the substance of the law. The last seven chapters describe the shift in the twentieth century, when judges, discredited as "oracles," became "lawmakers, not law-finders."

White profiles both state and federal appeals court judges, including many of the most famous justices of the United States Supreme Court. Each essay provides "an individual or group portrait," a discussion of leading decisions, and an analysis showing how decisions reflected contemporary ideas and influenced their development, as well. Single chapters will provide students interested in specific constitutional issues or cases with a broader judicial perspective, and teachers will find White's analysis helpful in comprehending the evolution of the tradition itself.

PERIOD STUDIES

Bailyn, Bernard. *The Ideological Origins of the American Revolution*. Cambridge: Harvard University Press, 1967.

This is a seminal work which has profoundly affected our understanding of the transforming role of ideas during the revolutionary period. Bailyn contends that the Revolution is still best understood as an ideological, constitutional, and political struggle. An "explosive amalgam of ideas" was generated by inflammatory words like slavery, corruption, and conspiracy, rather than by abstractions associated with natural rights philosophy or the Enlightenment. He focuses on the "logic of rebellion" and on the relationship between power and liberty. Bailyn concludes that it was primarily the colonial perception of a conspiracy against liberty fueling the engines of corruption that in the end propelled Americans into revolution. The "contagion of liberty" caused them to reexamine representation, consent, and fixed constitutions to define and limit government's "permissible sphere of action." Sovereignty must be shared, they concluded; it could not be the "monopoly of a single all-engrossing agency."

Bailyn's challenging study is an elaboration of a book-length introduction which appeared in the first of a projected four-volume collection of *Pamphlets of the American Revolution* (Cambridge: Harvard University Press, 1965). Although advanced students will profit from his superb analysis of ideas and may use selected chapters to good advantage, average students may be overwhelmed. Teachers, however, will find this to be a superb source from which to construct a fresh approach to the evolution of republican ideas.

Beth, Loren P. *The Development of the American Constitution, 1877–1917*. New York: Harper and Row, 1971. The New American Nation Series.

The problem during this period, Beth explains, was to adapt a Constitution which had flourished in a simple rural society, among a people suspicious of power and devoted to local control, to the needs of a complex urban industrial nation requiring more active government. In the process, constitutional revolution occurred. First, a Constitution intended to restrict government was used instead to enlarge the sphere and scope of government activity. Most importantly, accommodation to the fact of combination in business and labor accelerated the emergence of a supervisory role for the national government and a welfare function for the states. With a new interest in international activity, power shifted to the executive and the forces of war were centralized. In all of this, the Constitution was affected by a simultaneous revolution in political and constitutional thought associated with the impact of evolution and pragmatism in the social sciences.

Students will find Beth's study a useful supplement as a source on constitutional questions during the industrial and progressive periods. Teachers will find Beth helpful in explaining how important changes can occur without plan or purpose. The Court, he notes, was a reluctant accomplice which usually disapproved, often regretted, but finally could not resist the changes going on around it. By 1917, Americans had made fundamental changes in their institutions "almost in a fit of absent-mindedness."

Cortner, Richard C. *The Supreme Court and the Second Bill of Rights.* Madison: The University of Wisconsin Press, 1981.

Cortner describes the "nationalization" of civil liberties resulting from the extension of the Bill of Rights to protect individuals from state governments. Although the Bill of Rights was intended to restrict the powers of the national government only, since World War I many of its clauses have been used to curtail state and local governments. This has been a constitutional development of major importance. The nationalization process occurred gradually as a consequence of Court interpretations of the due process clause of the Fourteenth Amendment, not as a result of formal amendment. Thus, a second Bill of Rights was born in the application of the first to limit the powers of state governments. The transformation profoundly altered the relationship between the states and the central government.

Cortner's study is particularly valuable in showing the overwhelming significance of the Fourteenth Amendment in changing the constitutional basis for the protection of political and civil liberties. He explains the theoretical arguments for and against "incorporation" which have influenced the Supreme Court. The process attracted little public notice initially, but it became a matter of great public interest during the years of the Warren Court. Cortner describes the individuals and groups involved in specific cases from the 1870s through the period of "selective incorporation" in the 1960s, and he shows the impact of litigation on their lives.

Hyman, Harold, and William Wiecek. *Equal Justice Under the Law: Constitutional Development, 1835–1895.* New York: Harper and Row, 1982. The New American Nation Series.

The authors see this half-century as encompassing the greatest constitutional revolution in our history—a shift in the center of gravity from the states to the national government. Although this was not an era of political innovation, there were profound new forces at work which precipitated change. In the hands of an "unenterprising" Supreme Court, the central question became whether a Constitution based on the concept of limited government could meet the needs of a new economic order, power structure, and four million blacks whose status remained uncertain. The book considers constitutional questions involving slavery, states' rights, the end of state sovereignty, the shift from executive to legislative dominance after the war, the Fourteenth Amendment, and the role of the Court in accommodating law to the needs of an emerging national economy. Although the Court proved competent in more mundane affairs, the authors believe that it avoided problems involving blacks, women, and organized labor.

This is an extremely useful survey which will help teachers integrate constitutional issues into a general course of study from the antebellum period, through the Civil War and Reconstruction, to the acceleration of industrialization. Selected chapters may be used by students investigating more particular constitutional issues or studying the political climate in which those issues arose. An excellent twenty-two page bibliography directs students to additional works on specific topics.

Kurland, Phillip. *Watergate and the Constitution.* Chicago: University of Chicago Press, 1978.

Kurland's ten essays are not on the events of the Watergate affair themselves. Instead, they are wide-ranging discussions of constitutional issues which surfaced in connection with that scandal. He sees Watergate as a crisis resulting from the concentration of power in the executive. Although we survived the crisis, Kurland argues that we have yet to rid the constitutional system of the disease which infected it. No effective steps have been taken to prevent its recurrence, despite numerous assurances to the contrary. Each essay is informed, complex, provocative, and argumentative, and each contains an elaborate historical exposition of the topic at issue. They range from a consideration of Congress's powers of inquiry, executive privilege, the expansion of judicial power, and presidential appointments and pardons, to impeachment, the separation of powers, and checks and balances. Through it all, Kurland emphasizes the aggrandizement of executive power, the expansion of judicial authority, and the inadequacy of Congress to prevent those developments.

These essays are beyond the abilities of most students, but because they may be used independently of each other, advanced students should be encouraged to sample them. Teachers will find them revealing and perceptive, although they may not agree with the author's point of view. Taken together, the essays should prove valuable to teachers attempting to instruct their students in the constitutional aspects of a political scandal.

Murphy, Paul L. *The Constitution in Crisis Times, 1918–1969.* New York: Harper and Row, 1972. The New American Nation Series.

The author surveys twentieth-century constitutional development from World War I through the Warren Court. The shifting emphasis from protecting property rights to defending personal rights is the main theme of his study. It resulted, Murphy shows, from constant crisis, a pervasive tension between judicial activism and insensitivity, and conflicting efforts born in war itself and cold war to redefine the balance between liberty and order. The Court abandoned its traditional role as the major conservative force in government, becoming instead a "liberal quasi-legislative body." The content of the Constitution changed effectively as a result. The expanded role of government in economic affairs, for example, has been accompanied by the regulation of police, prosecutors, and trial judges. Rights of expression have been broadly defined. The right to vote, once under state supervision, is now controlled at the federal level. Government now intervenes to promote integration rather than to preserve segregation. Frequently critical of the Court's timidity in the face of public hysteria, Murphy observes that much of the Court's reputation is derived from undoing its own dirty work. The reversal of *Plessy v. Ferguson* (1896) by the *Brown* decision in 1954 is a case in point.

This survey has a wealth of detail to help students at work on constitutional cases, issues, or themes. It is especially strong in reconstructing the historical context of constitutional problems. The book also has an excellent fifty-five page bibliography.

Murphy, Paul L. *World War I and the Origin of Civil Liberties in the United States.* New York: W.W. Norton, 1979. The Norton Essays in American History.

Before 1917 there was no substantial body of law defining what rights were to be protected or how, despite public suspicion of federal power and a theoretical regard for the sanctity of personal freedoms under the Bill of Rights. Murphy argues that it was not until World War I that civil liberties emerged as a major national issue. Combined with Progressive inclinations to control social behavior, loyalty to the war effort was equated with liberal democratic reform at home and abroad, even as new restrictions "criminalized" many forms of expression, belief, and association. Extensive federal restraints precipitated the first major public debate over the distinction between liberty and license. As the federal government became "an active instrument of social control" in the emerging "surveillance state," new groups arose to "push the balance between liberty and order toward the former, not the latter," by defining liberties and defending them from federal suppression.

Murphy's study will prove valuable to teachers and advanced students interested in the evolving relationship between the powers of government and the rights of the people. It affords an excellent opportunity to examine how federal authority was used, ironically, to stifle liberty during a war for "democracy," and, secondly, why the defenders of civil liberties were often unable "to invoke successfully the symbolism of American freedom to protect the rights of unpopular Americans."

Newmyer, R. Kent. *The Supreme Court Under Marshall and Taney.* New York: Thomas Y. Crowell Company, 1968. The Crowell American History Series.

This is a remarkably concise and lucid explanation of major themes of constitutional development from 1801 to 1864. Against a framework defined by the limits and potential of judicial statesmanship, Newmyer distinguishes the role of the Marshall Court from its successor. Although the Marshall Court consolidated national power in service to capitalism, the Taney Court, despite its bolstering of slavery, sensed the threat to democracy arising from the alliance between property interests and government power. The Taney Court's suspicion of power was the basis for its advocacy of local responsibility and cultural pluralism. Despite these differences, Newmyer is far more impressed by similarities between the two Courts and by their joint contribution to the development of the Supreme Court as a broadly representative institution. Together, the Marshall and Taney Courts shaped the legal propositions that property was equated with liberty; that material progress was the accepted measure of achievement; and that government should serve individual and national growth by aiding capitalism. In the end, the Court formulated principles to bolster the free enterprise system through constitutional interpretation.

Newmyer's book is a very readable one hundred and fifty pages. It is perceptive at every turn, bringing clarity and coherence to the development of the Court and the Constitution. Students at most levels will profit enormously from this excellent short study.

Randall, James G. *Constitutional Problems Under Lincoln.* Revised edition. Urbana: University of Illinois Press, 1964.

Randall focuses on a basic problem facing American democracy. Although government must preserve the rights of its people, it must bear the obligation in wartime of preventing dissent from threatening destruction of the nation. As Lincoln put it, "Must a government, of necessity, be too strong for the liberties of its own people, or too weak to maintain its own existence?" Randall describes constitutional problems as legal formulations of concrete issues, not as abstract questions of theory. Specifically, he deals with complex problems involving war powers and impact on individual liberties, emancipation, the confiscation of property, and federal-state relations. Randall concludes that, measured against the rule of law, government during the Civil War was "conspicuous" for "its irregular and extra-legal characteristics." Lincoln's vast expansion of presidential power occurred without legal precedent or effective restraint by Congress or the Supreme Court. Yet, Lincoln's own "legal-mindedness" and "dislike of arbitrary rule" moderated the sometimes excessive zeal of his subordinates. Although frequently denounced as a dictator, Lincoln neither annihilated civil liberties nor established a dictatorship.

First published in 1926 and revised in 1951, Randall's book remains a superb introduction to the problems confronting a constitutional democracy at war with itself. Students may use selected chapters on specific problems to illustrate the fundamental dilemma as Lincoln perceived it.

Rossiter, Clinton. *1787: The Grand Convention.* New York: Mentor Books, 1966.

Describing 1787 as "the most fateful year in the history of the United States," Rossiter explores the Constitutional Convention as a case study in the political process of a constitutional democracy, in nation-building, and in "whether men are makers or wards of history." He begins by explaining the "setting," the "ills and remedies," and the "materials and choices" confronting the delegates. His second section describes the delegates, dividing them by region and providing at least a brief comment on each. In the third section, Rossiter details the work of the convention itself, beginning with the "nationalist assault" of the opening stages, through compromises and the working out of details. He concludes with an account of the finished product, the ratification controversy, the first years under the Constitution, and the later years of the Founding Fathers.

The book will be extremely useful to teachers and students reconstructing the work of the convention, analyzing the variety of conflicting interests at play, and detailing the compromises achieved by the delegates. Students will also find it invaluable in clarifying the historical context in which the convention took place. Among the important documents contained in the appendix are the Virginia and New Jersey Plans, and two reports from convention committees. Chapters can be used selectively to accommodate divergent interests and abilities among students. This is an excellent book with which to augment the study of any phase of the convention.

Rutland, Robert Allen. *The Birth of the Bill of Rights.* Revised edition. Boston: Northeastern University Press, 1983.

Rutland's purpose is to explain "how Americans came to rely on legal guarantees for their personal freedom." He begins with the English origins of American rights. The colonial achievement, seen in charters and legislative enactments, committed Americans to written laws and guarantees. One legislature imitated another, yet all worked from the same common-law tradition in similar circumstances, and their respective experiences influenced developing traditions elsewhere. Rutland explains that through elected representatives, the people of New England and New York adopted codes to protect their rights and property from arbitrary infringement. Experience with proprietary grants in other colonies demonstrated the wisdom of making grants explicit to ensure the rule of law approved by themselves, rather than the rule of other men over whom they had no control. Rutland concentrates on the evolution of the Bill of Rights from its seeds in state constitutions, the Constitutional Convention of 1787, the subsequent process of ratification, and finally the political maneuvering in Congress and out which resulted in adoption.

Rutland's highly readable study will help students understand the background of the Bill of Rights and the historical context in which it was adopted. The book may be used by students at most levels, and, if necessary, selected chapters may be used without destroying the book's continuity.

Smith, James Morton. *Freedom's Fetters: The Alien and Sedition Laws and American Civil Liberties.* Ithaca, New York: Cornell University Press, 1966.

Smith argues that between 1798 and 1801 the problem confronting the nation was to define the role of public criticism in a representative government. The failure of the Alien and Sedition Acts to silence Republican criticism of elected officials reinforced the new and revolutionary principle that government rests upon the consent of the governed. Federalists believed that the people's right to participate in government was limited to the election of the "good and wise." Committed to the concept of a ruling elite, they equated criticism aimed against them with attempted subversion of the Constitution and the overthrow of republican government. Republicans, however, believed that popular participation in government extended beyond voting, to the continuous, free, and public investigation of official conduct. The resulting controversy surrounding the Alien and Sedition Acts raised questions for the first time about the meaning of the First Amendment and focused attention on its definition as an essential ingredient in free government.

First published in 1956, Smith's study will help teachers compare two dominant ideas in the period. Historians since Smith have increasingly recognized in these countervailing views two varieties of republican thought rather than diametrically opposed views. Students will profit from Smith's discussion of the importance of free speech for free government and the evolution of freedom of the press from prior restraint, and from his analysis of an emerging conviction that the rights of the people are superior to the powers of government.

Storing, Herbert J., with the editorial assistance of Murray Dry. *What the Anti-Federalists Were For.* Chicago: University of Chicago Press, 1981.

Although disorganized and rarely in agreement, the Anti-federalists arrived at negative conclusions about the Constitution from a surprisingly positive set of principles. Like their Federalist opponents, they agreed that government was necessary to protect rights and that a limited, republican government afforded the best chance to accomplish this. Still, there was a continuous "tension"—a critical weakness—in their position. It was not that Anti-federalists failed to see the promise of America's republican future, but that instead they held back—doubtful—unable to join with Federalists in grasping it. Thus, they defended the *status quo* against innovation. They advocated the primacy of the states in a small republic with a homogeneous population. They resisted the apparent aristocratic tendency of the Constitution which endangered the "democracy" they perceived at the local level. Finally, they insisted on a bill of rights in this "consolidated" version of a federal system.

This slim volume of less than one-hundred pages is the introduction—here published separately—to Storing's multi-volumed collection of *The Complete Anti-Federalist,* which includes all substantial Anti-federalist writings in complete, original form, and with appropriate annotations. An appendix to the present volume lists the full contents of *The Complete Anti-Federalist.* In addition, major Anti-federalist ideas are keyed to specific writings in the larger collection.

Wood, Gordon S. *The Creation of the American Republic, 1776–1787.* Chapel Hill: University of North Carolina Press, 1969.

Wood's remarkable study has been instrumental in shaping our current understanding of republicanism as a revolutionary ideology. Beneath the process of constitution-making lay common assumptions about history, society, and politics which gave coherence to seemingly unrelated ideas. But the meaning of certain elements in America's distinctive political culture—liberty, democracy, virtue, and republicanism—changed between 1776 and 1787. More than the construction of new forms of government, Wood argues, Americans had built a new, modern form of politics. Their quarrels with Great Britain in the 1760s precipitated a deep discussion of political ideas. When war came, Americans translated those ideas into practice. Yet, the need to institutionalize their experience in revolution "accelerated and telescoped" intellectual development and exposed ambiguities and contradictions. By the 1780s, Wood concludes, the way was open to resolve the problems of American politics by the redefinition of political principles—a task made possible by the demands of justifying the new national Constitution.

Wood's analysis is brilliant, complex, and profound. It is an essential source for teachers who want to understand the Constitution as a product of republican ideology shaped by revolution. Its length will intimidate all but the most advanced students. Some chapters, however, carefully selected by teachers, can be used independently of others to supplement the work of more capable students.

Wood, Gordon S., ed. *The Confederation and the Constitution: The Critical Issues.* New York: Little, Brown and Company, 1973.

The seven essays in this collection offer valuable insights into the interpretive problems surrounding the formation of the Constitution. At the same time, they exemplify several major schools of historical thought on the subject. Indirectly, the articles help to clarify the distinction between republicanism—an ideology to which Americans in general were deeply committed—and democracy. Wood organizes the articles around three main questions. "What are the sources of the Constitutional Convention?" "What was the Federalist-Anti-federalist debate about?" "What was the relation of the Constitution to democracy?" Taken together, these questions reveal the complicated problems encountered in trying to assess the nature of the Constitution in its revolutionary context.

Wood's introduction offers an excellent historiographical survey of the literature concerning the writing of the Constitution. In his preface to each article he explains its place in the wider stream of opinion on the specific question at issue. The articles themselves, averaging twenty pages, are thoughtful, provocative, and frequently profound. They will be extremely useful to students with a solid preparation in the history of the period who are interested in understanding the Constitution as part of the broader revolutionary experience of eighteenth-century America. They will be especially valuable to those grappling with the relationship between republicanism and democracy.

CASE STUDIES

Baxter, Maurice G. *The Steamboat Monopoly: Gibbons v. Ogden, 1824.* New York: Alfred Knopf, 1972. The Borzoi Series in United States Constitutional History.

Baxter provides a brief analysis of the first great case involving the commerce clause of the Constitution. He describes the political and economic context in which the case arose and the long-range significance of the Supreme Court's decision. John Marshall ruled that a monopoly granted by the state of New York was unconstitutional because it conflicted with a federal statute. The decision rested upon a potentially broad definition of commerce. Yet, while the decision offended advocates of states' rights, in deference to them and to hold his Court together, the Chief Justice did not claim an exclusive national power over commerce. States retained authority in intrastate commerce. Marshall leaned toward, but avoided explicit approval of, the "silence of Congress" concept which would permit state action in the absence of federal legislation. As a result, it was the Court—not Congress—that fixed the boundaries separating national and state powers. Despite Marshall's statesmanlike decision against localism and monopoly, the basic issue of federalism remained unresolved, Baxter concludes. He explores reasons why the decision was not definitive and describes later cases which dealt with the commerce question.

Teachers and students examining the evolution of the Court's position on the commerce clause or the case in particular will find Baxter's provocative analysis rewarding. Each chapter is divided by sub-headings which make it easier to read.

Cortner, Richard C. *The Apportionment Cases.* Knoxville: University of Tennessee Press, 1970.

The principle of "one man, one vote" emerged from decisions in *Baker v. Carr* (1962) and *Reynolds v. Sims* (1964). As a result of these two cases, the federal courts took jurisdiction over state legislative apportionment. Consequently, there was a major shift of political power toward the nation's urban areas where most of the population now lives. These cases signified the Court's increased concern for constitutional guarantees of equality. From the white primary cases through the desegregation cases of the 1950s, the Court had separated equality in matters of race from the issue of unequal representation. The decision in *Baker v. Carr* was a "doctrinal breakthrough," extending the constitutional right of equality from the field of racial discrimination to the area of geographical discrimination and its political consequences. Cortner's study of the cases is enhanced by his focus on "litigating coalitions" and informal alliances that coalesced out of temporary common interests.

This is an excellent treatment of one of the most important constitutional principles to emerge in recent years. Cortner's analysis is clear and his narrative highly readable. Teachers may use it to augment study of the Constitution and the idea of representation, or in connection with the changing focus of the modern Supreme Court. Students will find it a valuable source of information when researching either of these topics.

Cortner, Richard C. *The Jones and Laughlin Case.* New York: Alfred Knopf, 1970. The Borzoi Series in United States Constitutional History.

The National Labor Relations Board brought suit against the Jones and Laughlin Steel Company in 1935 when it fired union men for engaging in union work. The Board viewed the case as a chance to test the constitutionality of the National Labor Relations Act. It hoped to resolve the controversy concerning New Deal efforts to define manufacturing enterprises as part of interstate commerce. So construed, the law invoked the commerce clause as the constitutional basis for regulating labor practices and compelling union recognition. The case, eventually joined with four others, illustrated the clash of constitutional views formulated in the nineteenth century with newer conceptions of the interdependence between capital and labor. The Court's decision in 1937, in the midst of FDR's court-packing effort, signified an acceptance of the New Deal's move toward a regulatory state. The Court abandoned its earlier role as censor of regulatory policies formulated by the President and Congress. By upholding the NLRA, moreover, the Court began to focus on issues of equality which have marked a host of cases since.

The Jones and Laughlin Case is readable and, though not a long book, packed with information. Teachers may use it to supplement instruction not only on the case itself, but also on the constitutional issues raised by the New Deal, judicial interpretation of the commerce power, the development of national regulation of the economy, and labor relations during the period. Students investigating any of these topics will find it an excellent source of information.

Dewey, Donald D. *Marshall versus Jefferson: The Political Background of Marbury v. Madison.* New York: Alfred Knopf, 1970. The Borzoi Series in United States Constitutional History.

Dewey argues that the Chief Justice's decision in the case of *Marbury v. Madison* to limit the Court's original jurisdiction was clearly out of step with the Federalist philosophy of the 1790s and contrary to Marshall's own brand of federalism. But the apparent aberration cannot be understood by reference to philosophical differences between Marshall and the President. Marshall and Jefferson despised each other, Dewey tells us, and only by considering their personal enmity and political realities of the time can Marshall's interpretation be explained. Deciding that Marbury was entitled to his commission as a Justice of the Peace, but ruling that the law empowering the Court to force its delivery was unconstitutional, Marshall sacrificed a tiny portion of original jurisdiction, but elevated the Court by setting a precedent for judicial review of federal law. The Chief Justice lectured the President for depriving Marbury of his rights. In the process, Marshall also established precedent for the judicial review of executive conduct. Even though historians have always emphasized the former, Dewey shows that Marshall's "tinkering" with the executive excited contemporaries even more.

Teachers will find a good deal of intriguing information to enliven standard classroom discussions of the case and its impact. For students, Dewey's highly readable study illustrates the fact that the rules of constitutional law cannot be understood by abstract reasoning alone. They must take into account political and economic factors which influence and shape the context in which those rules are derived and applied.

Fehrenbacher, Don E. *The Dred Scott Case: Its Significance in American Law and Politics.* New York: Oxford University Press, 1978.

Fehrenbacher describes his study as "More than a history of the Dred Scott case, though something less than a comprehensive history of the sectional conflict." He sees the case as "a point of illumination upon more than a century of American history." Using another image, he likens the case to "the neck of an hourglass" into which causes converge and out of which consequences emerge. The book deals with expansion and slavery, the course of litigation leading to the Supreme Court's decision, and the consequences of its judgment. Not only did it aggravate "an already bitter sectional controversy," but it determined to a large degree "the shape of the final crisis." The decision, "a work of unmitigated partisanship, polemical in spirit though judicial in language," was actually "more like an ultimatum than a formula for sectional accommodation." It remains a vivid example of how "vast judicial power . . . could be generated if political issues were converted . . . into constitutional issues."

The Dred Scott Case won a Pulitzer Prize in 1979. It contains almost six hundred pages of text and more than two hundred pages of notes. Students will find a condensed edition, *Slavery, Law, and Politics: The Dred Scott Case in Historical Perspective* (New York: Oxford, 1981), less formidable. Only half as long, with all documentation excluded, it contains the same chapters and themes. The author describes the shorter version as "less rich in detail but more to the point—suitable, I hope, for academic use and for the enlightenment of the general reader."

Garraty, John A., ed. *Quarrels That Have Shaped the Constitution.* New York: Harper & Row, 1964.

This collection of sixteen essays on important cases by various authors ranges in time from Garraty's own contribution, "The Case of the Missing Commissions" on *Marbury v. Madison,* to "The School Desegregation Case" by Alfred Kelly on *Brown v. Board of Education.* Collectively, the articles demonstrate the growth of the Supreme Court from a small tribunal, uncertain of its authority in an age particularly suspicious of federal power, to an aggressive agent for social reform acting in the name of the general welfare of the public. These cases show quite clearly, however, that great legal and constitutional questions are often raised by ordinary people pursuing their own self-interests, which are often petty and frequently insignificant to any besides themselves, until those concerns inspire major constitutional interpretations. So it was, for example, that the Court's most famous early assertion of judicial review occurred in a partisan political dispute involving an insignificant, would-be Justice of the Peace, William Marbury. As Garraty concludes, "such trivial arguments by men concerned with their own interests have often resulted in decisions that have shaken the foundations of American society."

These essays offer a fine introduction to the cases themselves and to the broader themes of constitutional development. Averaging fifteen to twenty pages in length, they may be read and studied with profit by most students. Teachers will find them useful for acquiring background for the development of specific activities.

Kluger, Richard. ***Simple Justice: The History of Brown v. Board of Education and Black America's Struggle for Equality.*** **New York: Alfred Knopf, 1976.**

Much more than a study of the *Brown* decision, Kluger's work is a history of twentieth-century racial discrimination in education. It emphasizes the efforts of the National Association for the Advancement of Colored People to devise a strategy to circumvent institutionalized segregation. Although discrimination had been sanctioned by the courts in countless proceedings, the NAACP eventually decided to attack its constitutionality on the grounds that separate facilities for blacks were inherently unequal. Kluger traces the development of that strategy through cases involving professional education for a few to the great question of equal opportunity in public elementary and secondary education for the many. The decision of the Court in 1954, a consolidated opinion on several cases involving school segregation, rested on the conviction that segregation violated black rights under the Fourteenth Amendment. Kluger believes that probably no case ever "affected more directly the minds, hearts, and daily lives of so many Americans." Already given a high place in "the literature on liberty," the *Brown* decision marked a turning point in race relations in the United States.

Kluger's massive study is more than eight hundred pages long—too long for assignment to any but the most committed students. It remains, however, the most comprehensive study of the issue. Teachers will find it helpful in showing how the law and people interact; how past and present social imperatives collide; and how the Court chose to define and extend equality of opportunity in public education.

Kutler, Stanley I. ***Privilege and Creative Destruction: The Charles River Bridge Case.*** **Philadelphia: J. B. Lippincott, 1971.**

This is an intriguing "tale of two bridges," one built in 1786, the other in 1828, both by private companies. Both were chartered by the Massachusetts legislature and ran close to each other between Boston and Charlestown. Technologically superior, the new bridge would become public after the Warren Bridge Company collected tolls for six years. The charter for this second bridge, however, interfered with exclusive privileges granted—and later extended—to the Charles River Bridge Company to collect tolls. As a result, the case involved claims that the second charter impaired the obligation of contracts and took private property—in the form of exclusive rights to collect tolls—for public use without compensation. In Kutler's view, the Court's decision to uphold the second charter amounted to the destruction of the Charles River Bridge Company's vested interest in favor of a beneficial change for the community, reflecting a creative process vital to ongoing progress. Hence the phrase, "creative destruction."

Teachers will be able to use this brief study in connection with a number of themes: the evolution of the contract clause from Marshall to Taney, the state's role in encouraging innovation for public benefit, the entrepreneurial spirit of the times which regarded private property as a dynamic rather than static institution, and the accommodation of law to technological and economic change. Any of those topics would be suitable for investigation by advanced students.

Lewis, Anthony. *Gideon's Trumpet.* New York: Random House, 1964.

This is the story of Clarence Earl Gideon, convicted of petty larceny and of breaking into and entering the Bay Harbor Poolroom in Panama City, Florida. Sentenced to five years in prison, Gideon claimed his conviction violated his rights to due process under the Fourteenth Amendment, because he had asked for, but been denied a court-appointed lawyer at his trial. The case eventually caused the Supreme Court in 1963 to overturn a precedent set twenty-one years earlier. Lewis presents a moving narrative of the entire legal process in the case from the commission of the crime to the Supreme Court's affirmation of Gideon's right to counsel. The case resulted in a major decision of the Warren Court extending federal protection to those accused of crimes prosecuted by the states. The decision illustrates the continuing process of incorporating the Bill of Rights through the Fourteenth Amendment, making them applicable to the states as well as the national government.

Because it was written in 1964, Lewis' account provides little analysis of the impact of the decision. Yet, students can use *Gideon's Trumpet* not only as a case study on the right to counsel during trial, but as a bridge to studying the subsequent extension of that right to other circumstances. After all, teachers might ask them, what good is the right to counsel during a trial, if that right was denied *before* the trial commenced? This highly readable and popular book makes fascinating reading and will appeal to students at most levels.

Magrath, C. Peter. *Yazoo: Law and Politics in the New Republic—The Case of Fletcher v. Peck.* Providence: Brown University Press, 1966.

The case of *Fletcher v. Peck* had its roots in fraudulent land speculation, and it became a gigantic political and constitutional problem. It scandalized Georgia, troubled Congress and the administrations of four Presidents, and divided the Republican Party. For the first time, Magrath observes, a large and well-organized pressure group lobbied a case to the Supreme Court and saw how the Court might be a source of valuable political and economic decisions. The Court employed the contract clause as a mechanism for protecting property rights. This clause provided a vital link, Magrath explains, between capitalism and constitutionalism as enterpreneurs sought protection from legislative interference. In a period when states were the source of most law regulating business, the contract clause became the chief restraint on state legislatures. Public grants, like private contracts, would be protected by it. Property rights thereby rose in the hierarchy of constitutional values, and the courts were obligated to invalidate state laws which tampered with contracts, public or private.

Magrath tells a fascinating and colorful story of fraud and bribery, law and political conflict, the courts and the Constitution. Teachers might use the eighty-six pages of appended documents to create an intriguing lesson inquiring into the meaning of the contract clause. The book can be valuable for students working on the relationship between government and people who owned—or speculated in—property.

Meyer, Howard N. *The Amendment that Refused to Die: Amendment XIV.* Boston: Beacon Press, 1978.

Meyer's episodic history focuses on Section One of what he calls the "Big Fourteen." He describes the framers of the Fourteenth Amendment as "draftsmen" or "founding fathers" of the "second constitution" after the Civil War, who intended to "consolidate" the gains of a "second revolution." Betrayal followed within a decade. Of necessity, then, a third revolution began. Its goal was not "the prospect of a third constitution," but a "return to the second constitution as written." Gains were "wrested, bit by bit, from the changing membership of the United States Supreme Court." By 1970, that revolution had established the Fourteenth Amendment as "the 'law' of the land." Meyer asks whether its redemption came too late.

Meyer's thesis is provocative, although his claim that the Amendment's authors clearly intended to protect from state abuse "the rights Americans had won from their central government in 1789" is debated by other historians. Teachers might compare Meyer on this point with Raoul Berger, *Government By Judiciary: The Transformation of the Fourteenth Amendment* (Cambridge: Harvard University Press, 1977). Meyer disagrees with those who credit the Warren Court with granting "new rights," rather than reaffirming those intended by the Amendment all along. Richard Cortner's study, *The Supreme Court and the Second Bill of Rights,* discussed elsewhere in this Bibliography, offers a different historical perspective.

This book was nominated for a Pulitzer Prize when it was first published in 1973. Students will find its thirty-three brief chapters to be lively, readable, and memorable for their vivid sketches of sometimes obscure historical figures. The book may be assigned as a whole, but selected chapters will prove just as useful.

Pritchett, C. Herman, and Alan F. Westin, eds. *The Third Branch of Government: Eight Cases in Constitutional Politics.* New York: Harcourt, Brace and World, Inc., 1963.

The editors have assembled eight case studies written by various authors to depict the tendencies of the Supreme Court since 1937 and to explore the politics of judicial review. The Court has become more liberal since then, Pritchett and Westin argue, and has shifted its emphasis from a primary concern with property to a "jurisprudence of status" in which the dominant issues involve the quality of life. The cases chosen, therefore, involve the central issues of liberty and equality—not property. They deal with free speech, religion, Cold War security, and federal-state relations. Only two are devoted to clearly economic issues, and the section on "Sunday closings" offers a fascinating mixture of commerce and religion. The "status agenda" includes the problems of discrimination against minority groups, freedom of expression and association, and due process in criminal proceedings. With a shift in the posture of the Court, the attackers and defenders of the Court have changed positions, too, reflecting fundamental changes in most aspects of the nation's life.

The case studies are well designed for students. Constructed to show the complexity of the point in question, each essay includes background information, descriptions of conflict, strategic dilemmas confronting private and public groups, the course of litigation, and an analysis of the impact of the Court's decision. Averaging thirty-five pages, these detailed narratives are interspersed with edited documents to aid student inquiry.

Stites, Francis N. *Private Interest and Public Gain: The Dartmouth College Case, 1819.* Amherst: University of Massachusetts Press, 1972.

The Dartmouth College case, arising out of a controversy over control of the institution, was vital to nineteenth-century economic development. Stites provides a crisp explanation of the context in which the case occurred, carefully reconstructing the background, unraveling the confusing record of conflict between the college's president and its trustees, and describing the partisan intrigues and personality clashes of the preceding years. Having explained three years of litigation, Stites concludes with an analysis of the Supreme Court's decision and its subsequent modifications. The Court ruled that the college's charter of incorporation was a contract and that state law attempting to change it was unconstitutional. The decision brought private charters within the scope of the contract clause in the Constitution. It restricted state power and rendered the corporation useful to the needs of a developing economy. A reverence for property rights and a fear that states might abridge them prompted the Marshall Court to expand the contract clause into a shield for vested rights.

This slim volume of 100 pages is tightly written and cogently reasoned. Close reading will yield greater comprehension of the wedding of private property rights and public welfare. It is an excellent case study of the trend toward the protection of property based on the contract clause, and a valuable source for students investigating the evolution of constitutional protection of private economic interests.

Westin, Alan F. *The Anatomy of a Constitutional Law Case.* New York: The Macmillan Company, 1958.

Westin's case study is a "documentary portrait" of *Youngstown Sheet Tube Co. v. Sawyer* from its origins in a labor dispute to the aftermath of the Supreme Court's decision. The case resulted from Truman's seizure of steel mills in 1952, and it raised important constitutional questions about the inherent powers of the President. Westin's brief chapters couple a short introduction with key documents edited to illustrate how legal conflicts are shaped by other forces; how a case makes its way to the Supreme Court; how legal strategies affect the development of constitutional principles; how the conduct of the other branches affects the Supreme Court; and how the justices resolve the issues confronting them. The documents include excerpts from newspaper articles, presidential messages, speeches, transcripts, and legal briefs. Helpful aids include a chronology of the case and profiles of the justices. Following a three-page comment of his own, Westin ends with a set of twelve thought-provoking questions to spur discussion and closer examination of key aspects of the case.

Westin's book is an excellent example of how teachers may instruct students in constitutional procedure—and in the use of primary sources—through carefully selected documents from divergent sources. For a later, more complete history of the case itself, students and teachers may consult Maeva Marcus, *Truman and the Steel Seizure Case: The Limits of Presidential Power* (New York: Columbia University Press, 1977).

DOCUMENTS AND SOURCES

Bardolph, Richard, ed. *The Civil Rights Record: Black Americans and the Law, 1849–1970.* New York: Thomas Y. Crowell Company, 1970.

Bardolph has edited more than four hundred and fifty documents from divergent sources concerning race relations and public policy. He treats the years before 1865 briefly, devoting more attention to the "first shock of freedom," followed by "fading hopes" at the end of the nineteenth century. While "the color line held" through the 1930s, Bardolph sees "reviving hopes" from 1938 to 1954. The last section, three times longer than any of the others, examines the "progress, stalemate or reaction" from 1954 to 1970. Each section begins with a sample of contemporary opinion on racial ideology and continues with views from the White House, national party platforms, state and national legislation, and court opinions. Bardolph provides brief introductions to each section, as well as extensive comments that link documents and convey clearly the evolution of the particular theme under consideration. This commentary makes the book a valuable historical survey of race relations which is generously interspersed with excerpts from primary sources, rather than a simple collection of documents with headnotes.

The Civil Rights Record can be used to great advantage by students investigating the history of race relations or looking for short, but illuminating sources. Teachers interested in using primary sources to add substance to their analyses of racial issues or in connection with a specific theme will welcome Bardolph's collection.

Borden, Morton, ed. *The Antifederalist Papers.* Lansing, Michigan: Michigan State University Press, 1965.

Noting that the views of the Anti-federalists have been obscured because of the success of the Constitution they opposed, Borden presents here a representative cross section of Anti-federalist thought grouped in the same format as *The Federalist.* The eighty-five essays, varying in length from one to five pages, are drawn from newspapers, pamphlets, and letters. Although half of them remain anonymous, the others were penned by such noted figures as George Mason, Richard Henry Lee, Patrick Henry, and George Clinton. The *Papers* include criticism of the Constitution as "A Dangerous Plan of Benefit Only to the Aristocratick Combination." The apprehension of aristocratic rule is a dominant theme reflected in attacks on the lack of a Bill of Rights, "the

President as Military King," and on "Representation and Internal Taxation." The essays also demonstrate fundamental differences among the Anti-federalists themselves. Whereas Henry sees the scale of representation as inadequate, for example, Lee worries that no system could be truly representative of the people. Such "internal tensions" indicate not only the disparity of views held by Antifederalists, but also the complexity of thought on issues central to the experiment in republican government.

Borden's brief introduction to each essay identifies its author, if known, and summarizes its main point. The collection will be especially useful for students and teachers seeking a comparative perspective on the issues which divided contemporaries.

Commager, Henry Steele, ed. *Documents of American History.* Two volumes. Ninth edition. Englewood Cliffs, New Jersey: Prentice-Hall, Inc., 1973.

This is an indispensable reference and learning tool. In order to illustrate the course of American history from the age of discovery to the present, Commager has selected documents essential to an understanding of American development. Defining "document" in a narrow sense, selections are limited to those of an "official or quasi-official character." Consequently, students and teachers will find laws, presidential messages, court decisions, and speeches. Essential documents such as the decision in *Marbury v. Madison* are complemented by others illustrating broader trends. As a result, readers will find charters, excerpts from the Lincoln-Douglas debates and similar documents which "serve as a point of departure" for the study of major trends or which exemplify some phase of our social life.

This is an extremely accessible collection of important documents. Each entry is prefaced by a brief introduction and bibliographical references. Teachers seeking greater use of primary sources will find these two volumes invaluable. They contain not only important documents in constitutional history, but others which illuminate the context in which that development occurred. For students, the documents provide a wealth of information beyond that available in texts. In addition, they offer "evidence" which may be used to substantiate student writing on historical questions. Volume I includes 345 documents and covers the period to 1898. Volume II moves from 1898 onward and contains 350 documents.

Cooke, Jacob, ed. *The Federalist.* Middletown, Connecticut: Wesleyan University Press, 1961.

When New York newspapers became filled with objections to the newly written Constitution, Alexander Hamilton decided to defend it with detailed explanations of its provisions. Addressed to the people of New York by "Publius," the essays by Hamilton, James Madison, and John Jay were intended to secure support for ratification. Quite aside from their immediate purpose, these eighty-five essays constitute "the most significant contribution Americans have made to political philosophy."

Cooke's definitive edition is based upon original manuscripts and takes into account revisions made by earlier editors. Extensive notes show variations in passages and words in previous editions. Explanatory footnotes identify references made by the authors to eighteenth-century political works which were well known to their audience, but not to modern readers. Cross-references will help students and teachers find other essays in the collection which deal with the same subject. Cooke's introduction offers a publication history of these papers, and he attempts to establish the authorship of disputed essays.

Modern students will find the essays difficult and complicated, but they will profit from a close reading of selected numbers chosen with care by the teacher. The essays provide an opportunity to analyze primary sources which are essential to an understanding of the Constitution and its underlying principles, and to study the evolution of republican thought in its practical political context.

Farrand, Max, ed. *The Records of the Federal Convention of 1787.* Four Volumes. New Haven: Yale University Press, 1966.

First published in 1911, then revised in a four-volume edition in 1937, Farrand's *Records* are the essential sources upon which our knowledge of the Constitutional Convention is based. In addition to the official *Journal* kept secret until 1819, these include the invaluable notes of James Madison, the recollections of Robert Yates, and the fragmentary records of others such as Rufus King. The records are arranged chronologically to provide a day-by-day account of the work of the Convention. There are no subject headings, but entries are cross-referenced in footnotes and there is an exhaustive general index. A special index refers to every clause in the Constitution and so enables teachers and students to trace the origin and development of a particular clause. Farrand supplements these with hundreds of pages of documents dating from 1787 through 1836. They include private correspondence, contributions to the press, public speeches, and debates in legislatures and conventions. A new, fifth volume of recently discovered documents and correcting errors in the earlier editions will be published in connection with the bicentennial of the Constitution.

This is an invaluable research tool for teachers and students alike. In particular, students can use the *Records* to trace the history of specific clauses, procedures, or compromises. Those interested principally in Madison's records may consult his *Notes of Debate in the Federal Convention of 1787,* edited in one volume by Adrienne Koch (Athens, Ohio: Ohio University Press, 1966).

Kutler, Stanley I., ed. *The Supreme Court and the Constitution: Readings in American Constitutional History.* Third edition. Boston: Houghton Mifflin Company, 1984.

The purpose of this casebook is to provide students with abridged versions of Supreme Court decisions which illustrate the development of the American constitutional tradition. The cases are arranged chronologically under standard period headings, and within each period they are arranged topically. Each entry begins with a headnote describing the historical and constitutional setting for the case. Some headnotes give factual background of the case, and an assessment of the relationship between the case in point and subsequent controversies. The length of each excerpt ranges from two to ten pages. Each selection has been made because of the editor's belief that it has "long-standing significance for constitutional law." Even though it is weighted toward cases dealing with economic issues, the collection as a whole deals with many of the major cases, Supreme Court decisions, and constitutional issues likely to concern most teachers and students involved in general survey classes.

Kutler's collection is readily available and easy to use. Teachers can assign the readings in class to supplement the study of specific constitutional cases or issues, or they can link several cases to create a lesson for students on a specific theme of constitutional development. Students at most levels can make use of it, and those researching the Supreme Court decisions which are included will find it especially convenient.

Smith, James Morton, and Paul L. Murphy, eds. *Liberty and Justice: A Historical Record of American Constitutional Development.* Two volumes. Revised edition. New York: Alfred Knopf, 1965.

The editors have brought together excerpts from public papers and speeches; public documents including laws, resolutions, and amendments; letters; manifestos; and a broad sampling of judicial opinion related to the development of representative government and individual freedom. The first volume, containing 111 documents, treats American constitutional development to 1869, from the origins of constitutional government through its greatest internal challenge in the Civil War. The second volume has 184 documents. It begins with constitutional attempts to protect black rights and ends with the Supreme Court and Congress returning to that unfinished task in the late 1950s and early 1960s. Smith and Murphy show why the process took so long: how attention was deflected to other interests; how progressives emphasized public needs over personal property rights; how the New Deal consolidated the trend towards big government; and how times of actual war and Cold War forced Americans to reassess the relationship between liberty and equality.

This set is designed for classroom use. The great variety of sources indicates the wide range of constitutional history. As a whole, they portray the evolution of an agrarian republic into an urban industrial society and show the transformation of the United States into a world power. The editors provide a brief introduction to each chapter. Teachers may choose relevant documents to provide a constitutional perspective on almost any subject dealt with in their survey classes.

BIBLIOGRAPHICAL GUIDES

Hall, Kermit L., ed. *A Comprehensive Bibliography of American Constitutional and Legal History, 1896–1979.* Five volumes. Millwood, New York: Kraus International Publications, 1984.

This is indeed a comprehensive, exhaustive bibliography of works published during the eighty-four years indicated. The entries are not annotated, but they are listed in logical topics and sub-topics so that a working bibliography on any subject can be developed quickly. Extensive indices and other reference aids are provided. This is the definitive bibliographic source for the period it covers. Because the set of five volumes costs $575, it will be found most commonly in libraries of law schools and universities.

Mason, Alpheus T., and D. Grier Stephenson, Jr., eds. *American Constitutional Development.* Arlington Heights, Illinois: AHM Publishing Corporation, 1977. Goldentree Bibliographies in American History Series.

Concise and easy to use, this bibliography is intended to hold the middle ground between the brief lists found in texts and the long bibliographies in which individual titles are lost in the sheer numbers. The entries include significant journal articles and dissertations as well as books. The bibliography contains just over three thousand entries arranged in categories such as general sources, origins, chronological periods, political institutions, doctrines and politics, the franchise and political process, and travel and expatriation.

McCarrick, Earlean M. *U.S. Constitution: A Guide to Information Sources.* Detroit: Gale Research Company, 1980. Volume 4 in the American Government and History Information Guide Series.

This guide briefly summarizes the topic of each entry in a single paragraph of two or three sentences. Divided into twelve chapters, it covers general sources, the background of the Constitution, the period of the Constitutional Convention and early years of the new republic, general interpretive works, basic principles, the Articles of the Constitution, and the amendments. The guide contains helpful author, title, and subject indices.

Millett, Stephen M., ed. *A Selected Bibliography of American Constitutional History.* Santa Barbara, California: Clio Press, Inc., 1975.

This is a bibliography of secondary works on the Constitution. By looking up the article and section number of the Constitution, the reader will find a list of published works on that subject. With slightly over one thousand entries, the bibliography contains books, articles, and a list of legal journals. In addition to the major focus on specific parts of the Constitution, Millett includes sections on the drafting and ratification of the Constitution, major Supreme Court cases, judicial biographies, and "extrajudicial" constitutional history about the impact of major events.

Stephenson, Jr., D. Grier. *The Supreme Court and the American Republic: An Annotated Bibliography.* New York: Garland Publishing Company, 1981.

Each of the more than thirteen hundred entries contains a brief annotation of a sentence or two. Stephenson's emphasis is on the powers of government and the limitations on them as determined by the Constitution and the laws. As a result, while the bibliography is comprehensive, Stephenson avoids the temptation "to stray too far from the Court itself." He also emphasizes books that are readily available. Sections four and five contain descriptions of key cases arranged chronologically in seven periods from 1789 to the 1970s, with analyses and other materials annotated for each era.

INDEX